My Turn To Learn

An Up-To-Date Guide
For Parents of Babies and Children With Hearing Loss

SUSAN LANE • LORI BELL • TERRY PARSON-TYLKA

ILLUSTRATED BY KARINN PEARSON

Bright*futures*
for Children

BC Family Hearing Resource Centre
A program for families with young deaf and hard of hearing children
www.bcfamilyhearing.com

Parents whose young child has just been diagnosed with hearing loss need a resource and communication guide that addresses the many concerns and questions they have. They need information about successful methods for developing communication. They would also welcome ideas and experiences from other parents who have gone through the challenges they are about to face. Above all, they want their child to communicate effectively and develop good self-esteem. *My Turn To Learn* is designed to help parents do just that.

What parents and professionals said about the first edition of *My Turn To Learn* ...

"*My Turn To Learn* is a wonderful source of information for families. I wish we had it when our son was little! I often lend my copy to families of kids who have speech and language difficulties, even if they don't have a hearing loss. I look forward to seeing the second edition. I think the information on advocating for your child and the early literacy ideas will be very helpful for families. It's so great that this book was written by the people who are on the 'front lines' — out there working with our kids. They have a wealth of experience and practical information which is so valuable for parents."

Teresa Kazemir, Parent
Former President of the Parent Branch of
the Canadian Hard of Hearing Association
Speech/Language Pathologist

"*My Turn to Learn* is a wonderful resource for parents and for community professionals concerned with hearing loss in infants and young children. Hearing parents of deaf or hard of hearing children need access to a range of information that can help them understand their child's hearing loss, communication needs and strategies that will support their child's communication in the best ways possible. In a field that is characterized with complex and often contradictory information, *My Turn to Learn* serves as an invaluable tool to help parents make the very best decisions on behalf of themselves and their children. It should be recommended reading for all parents with a deaf or hard of hearing child."

Dana Brynelsen
Provincial Advisor to the Infant Development Program
British Columbia, Canada

"What a wonderful summary of all that we learned in our many years at the Elks Family Hearing Resource Centre (now BC Family Hearing Resource Centre). I especially appreciate the honest quotes of other parents. It's comforting to know that our feelings (whatever these may be) are okay — and to know that we are not alone."

Parent

"*My Turn To Learn* will lower your anxiety and feelings of helplessness, and guide you through the early stages of establishing communication with your child; then move on to becoming your child's partner in his early language development, and becoming effective communicators with each other."

Parent

MY TURN TO LEARN —

An Up-To-Date Guide for Parents of Babies and Children with Hearing Loss
(second edition)

by Susan Lane • Lori Bell • Terry Parson-Tylka

Illustrations by Karinn Pearson

Published by
BC Family Hearing Resource Centre
15220 – 92nd Avenue
Surrey, British Columbia
Canada V3R 2T8
604-584-9108 (TTY)
604-584-2827 (Voice)
1-877-584-2827 (Toll Free)
604-584-2800 (Fax)
web: www.bcfamilyhearing.com
email: info@bcfamilyhearing.com

ISBN: 0-9680964-0-9

Orders and Inquiries:
Bauhinea Press
1209 Madison Avenue
Burnaby, British Columbia
Canada V5C 4Y4
Phone: 604-298-1391
Email: bauhinea@gmail.com

ABOUT THE AUTHORS

Susan Lane

Susan Lane is the Director of the BC Family Hearing Resource Centre and has worked there since 1983. She was instrumental in developing the Parent Training and Support programs at the BC Family Hearing Resource Centre and facilitated a support and information group for parents with deaf and hard of hearing children for over 20 years. She has a Master's Degree in Communication Sciences and Disorders from the University of Montana.

Lori Bell

Lori Bell has worked at the BC Family Hearing Resource Centre since 1991. She has a Master's Degree in Sciences from the School of Audiology and Speech Sciences at the University of British Columbia. An entry level course for Visual Language Interpreters and volunteering with deaf adults led to Lori's interest in facilitating communication for families with young deaf and hard of hearing children.

Terry Parson-Tylka

Terry Parson-Tylka is a certified Teacher of the Deaf and Hard of Hearing with a Master's Degree in Special Education and Early Childhood from the University of British Columbia. She has taught deaf and hard of hearing children since 1974, in both oral and signing programs. She has been with the BC Family Hearing Resource Centre since 1989 and immensely enjoys working with infants, toddlers and preschoolers, their families, and community service providers throughout BC.

ABOUT THE ILLUSTRATOR

Karinn Pearson

Karinn Pearson has been drawing and painting since she was a toddler. She has won many awards for her art work and is currently living in Santa Cruz, California.

ACKNOWLEDGEMENTS

First and foremost we are deeply indebted to our team at the BC Family Hearing Resource Centre for their creative ideas, helpful suggestions, and support: Cathy Chow, Judy Chrastina, Dyan Spear, Nicola Swain, Noreen Simmons, Kristyn Payne, Karen Jackson, Robyn Church, Linda Spencer, Amanda Curry, Ellen Peterson, Val Matthews, Cathy Cruickshank, and our fabulous proof-reader, Cindy Adams.

We also want to thank the many families we have worked with who shared their experiences, opinions, and feelings with us as they faced the new challenge of parenting a young child with a hearing loss. We are constantly inspired by their courage and strength. We appreciated the feedback about our first edition that we received from parents attending our parent group meetings over the past few years. We especially appreciated the encouragement, insight, and suggestions for changes and additions from the parents who carefully reviewed our first edition as we prepared for our second: Sian Pitman, Sarah Lecky and Teresa Kazemir.

Several audiologists provided us with invaluable technical information, including Laurie Usher and Anna Van Maanen from BC Children's and Women's Hospital, Ann Marie Newroth from the BC Early Hearing Program, Anne Caulfield from the Vancouver Island Health Authority., and Kristine Juck, BC Children's Hospital Cochlear Implant team.

For their valuable and thoughtful comments, we gratefully acknowledge Arlene Stredler-Brown, Director of the Colorado Home Intervention Program, Dr. Janet Jamieson, Associate Professor & Director, Program in Education of the Deaf and Hard of Hearing, Faculty of Education-University of British Columbia, Dana Brynelsen, Provincial Advisor for the Infant Development Program, Carolyn Graves, Team Leader of Hearing Loss Team- Sunny Hill Health Centre for Children, and Teresa Kazemir, Past President, Canadian Hard of Hearing Association — BC Parents' Branch and Speech/Language Pathologist.

For their important contribution of expertise and time, we are grateful to our Board of Directors as well as our current Board Executive — Dr. Charles Laszlo, Sally Hurst, Doug McKinnon, and Carol Briner.

Our heartfelt thanks to the Benevolent and Protective Order of the **Elks of Canada** and the **Ladies of the Royal Purple** for their ongoing support of the BC Family Hearing Resource Centre through their national **Elks and Royal Purple Fund for Children** and through additional support at the Lodge level in British Columbia. The Elks and Royal Purple started our programs in 1983 and have continued to be our partners for over two decades. Special thanks go to Elks and Royal Purple members Gary Gee, Sally Hurst, Eleanor Scott, and Bob Baker.

Many thanks to the **CKNW Orphans Fund** for providing us with the financial support to publish our second edition of *My Turn to Learn*.

We thank the BC Ministry of Children and Family Development for continuing to help fund our important services for children; special thanks to Monte Hardy for his encouragement.

To our publishing and printing consultants, Ben and Amy Ho of Bauhinea Press, we appreciate their patience over the last two years and the tremendous care they put into our book. Ben and Amy recognized the importance of this book as they are parents of an amazing young woman who is profoundly deaf — Rosalind.

To our editors, Margaret and Dwight Lane, we want them to know that we might never have attempted this second edition without knowing they were there to assist us — again. We offer them our deepest gratitude for their expertise, advice, and the hundreds of hours you devoted to this project. Finally, we want to thank our families for their love and encouragement.

Susan Lane, Lori Bell, Terry Parson-Tylka

CONTENTS

Acknowledgements

Introduction
 About This Book
 How To Use This Book
 About the BC Family Hearing Resource Centre

PART I: GETTING STARTED

Chapter 1
 After the Diagnosis: Coping 3
Chapter 2
 Making Initial Decisions...17
Chapter 3
 Common Causes and Types of Hearing Loss.............................27
Chapter 4
 Hearing Tests and Results: Working Together With Your
 Pediatric Audiologist 33
Chapter 5
 Getting Started With Hearing Aids....................................51
Chapter 6
 Learning More About Hearing Aids....................................73
Chapter 7
 Cochlear Implants 93
Chapter 8
 Bringing My Child's Attention to Sound and
 Making Sound Meaningful 109
Chapter 9
 Observing My Child's Communication.............................123
Chapter 10
 Responding Positively to My Child's Attempts
 to Communicate 133
Chapter 11
 Getting Close to Communicate 145
Chapter 12
 Using Appropriate Rate and Intensity In Speech 151
Chapter 13
 Using Expression to Encourage Communication...................159

Chapter 14
    Deciding to Use Signs 165

PART II: BECOMING PARTNERS

Chapter 15
    Following My Child's Lead in Play and Interest 179
Chapter 16
    Modifying the Length and Complexity of My Message 187
Chapter 17
    Encouraging Turn-Taking 199
Chapter 18
    Questions, Commands and Commenting 205
Chapter 19
    Modelling Specific Sounds, Words, and
    Sentence Formations 219

PART III: MOVING FORWARD IN CONVERSATIONS

Chapter 20
    Expanding My Child's Language 237
Chapter 21
    Using Prompting 245
Chapter 22
    Helping to Repair Conversation Breakdowns 253
Chapter 23
    Advocating 269

PART IV: PROMOTING COMMUNICATION AND LITERACY IN ROUTINES

Chapter 24
    Ideas for Home, Play, and Away 293

A Few Last Words 339

Appendices:

    Appendix A: Helpful Resources 341

    Appendix B: Parent-to-Parent Support Network 351

    Appendix C: Services 353

    Appendix D: Glossary 355

    Appendix E: A Parent's Journal 363

    Appendix F: Learning to Listen and Communicate
       — From a Child's Point of View 369

INTRODUCTION

About This Book
How To Use This Book
About the BC Family Hearing Resource Centre

ABOUT THIS BOOK

Being a parent is not always easy. Being a parent of a deaf or hard of hearing child brings new and different challenges to an already complex job.

Because you are a parent of a deaf or hard of hearing child, there will be times when you feel a range of powerful emotions — from frustration to pride and back again. **You are not alone.** In this guide we have included concerns, questions, ideas and experiences that parents of deaf and hard of hearing children have shared with us. You will also find information and successful methods that staff members at the BC Family Hearing Resource Centre have developed through their work with families of deaf and hard of hearing children over the past twenty years.

Throughout this guide, we ask you to keep in mind these important thoughts:

- Your child is a unique and special individual. There is no one quite like him or her in this whole world.

- You are also a unique and special person.

- Together, you and your child create a unique and special relationship that no one else can duplicate.

- You, as a parent, are in the best position to know who your child is, what he needs, and how best to help him grow and learn and develop into a happy, well-adjusted and responsible adult.

This book was written for you — the parent of a child who is deaf or hard of hearing. It is a resource to help you and members of your family learn ways to build good communication with your child. Good communication is crucial for the development of your child's self-esteem.

The ideas in this book promote the development of positive self-esteem while at the same time building communication skills. In this way, as you communicate with your child, you give him important messages that help him feel: I am loved and cared about. I am a good person. I am important.

HOW TO USE THIS BOOK

This book contains ideas from parents of deaf and hard of hearing children, as well as from deaf and hard of hearing adults, teachers of the deaf and hard of hearing, speech and language pathologists, and early childhood educators from the BC Family Hearing Resource Centre Program.

This book is —

- **A guide** to aid you in planning ways to help your child develop communication skills, rather than a "cookbook" to be followed.

- **A resource** to go to when you want information in a particular area, rather than a book to be read from cover to cover in strict order.

- **A place to begin**, a source of ideas and suggestions for you to think and talk about with other family members, parents and professionals, rather than the place to end your search for the "right answers."

We hope this book will inspire you and support you in your efforts. We welcome your feedback about the information this guide offers you and about what

From a parent:
"This book is a wonderful summary of what we've learned in our years at the BC Family Hearing Resource Centre. I especially appreciate the honest quotes of other parents. It's comforting to know that our feelings (whatever these may be) are okay — and to know that we're not alone. Parents need to remember in reading through the book that they don't have to do everything it suggests right now, today. It takes time and practice to move through the process of helping your young child to communicate with others. This book is an invaluable guide — one to read and study by yourself or with the professionals who work with your family."

other areas you would like to have included in future publications from the BC Family Hearing Resource Centre.

ABOUT THE BC FAMILY HEARING RESOURCE CENTRE

The BC Family Hearing Resource Centre, located in British Columbia, was established in 1983. Our focus is on a family-centred, early-intervention program that is committed to individual communication choices. It provides support and resources to deaf and hard of hearing children, their families and community service providers throughout BC.

In addition to comprehensive services to "local" families living within commuting distance of the Centre, we have an Outreach Program which offers a range of services designed to meet the unique needs of families living in smaller communities and rural areas throughout BC. Because we appreciate the invaluable support parents offer to one another, we have established a Parent-to-Parent Support Network for families of deaf and hard of hearing children as a way of connecting families with similar concerns and experiences.

A more detailed description of the Parent-to-Parent Support Network is included in the appendices. For more information about any of our services, please contact our Centre.

BC FAMILY HEARING RESOURCE CENTRE
15220 92nd Avenue
Surrey, BC V3R 2T8
Canada
Telephone: 604-584-9108 (TTY)
             604-584-2827 (Voice)
             604-584-2800 (Fax)
Web: www.bcfamilyhearing.com
Email: info@bcfamilyhearing.com

PART I: GETTING STARTED

Like other parents of young deaf and hard of hearing children, you recognize the importance of helping your child develop communication. But you may wonder how to begin. Part I of this book discusses the important skills that, like building blocks, will form the foundation of good communication with your child. The initial chapters deal with the first challenges you may be facing: making decisions about sign language, cochlear implants and hearing aids. You'll also learn to identify your child's first communication attempts, how you can encourage these attempts, and how to make your message more available to your child.

Chapter 1: After the Diagnosis: Coping … 3

Chapter 2: Making Initial Decisions … 17

Chapter 3: Common Causes and Types of Hearing Loss … 27

Chapter 4: Hearing Tests and Results: Working Together With Your Pediatric Audiologist … 33

Chapter 5: Getting Started with Hearing Aids … 51

Chapter 6: Learning More About Hearing Aids … 73

Chapter 7: Cochlear Implants … 93

Chapter 8: Bringing My Child's Attention to Sound and Making Sound Meaningful … 109

Chapter 9: Observing My Child's Communication … 123

Chapter 10: Responding Positively to My Child's Attempts to Communicate … 133

Chapter 11: Getting Close to Communicate … 145

Chapter 12: Using Appropriate Rate and Intensity In Speech … 151

Chapter 13: Using Expression to Encourage Communication ... *159*

Chapter 14: Deciding to Use Signs ... *165*

CHAPTER 1

AFTER THE DIAGNOSIS: COPING

Grieving 3
Steps to Take in Adapting to Loss 7
When Is Grieving Finished? 13
Getting Help 14

GRIEVING

When we mourn a death, we are mourning the loss of a loved one. When hearing parents learn their child is deaf or hard of hearing, they often go through a similar experience of grieving. They are suffering over the loss of the "perfect" (hearing) child they thought they would have. They grieve over the loss of the dreams they had for that child.

Many deaf parents report feeling happiness and joy upon learning their child is deaf, too. These parents, then, do not experience grieving.

Feelings You May Experience

Parents tell us they often felt they were going crazy during the early stages of mourning and believed no one else had ever reacted in this way. Here are some common feelings that many experience:

Sadness

- May be accompanied by crying.

  "I spent the first two weeks crying, almost constantly."

Anger

- Parents may become angry at a spouse, feeling that the other person is not demonstrating emotions in the same way. *"Doesn't he feel anything?"* If one person is primarily responsible for taking the child to appointments, he or she may feel angry at "carrying the whole load."

"My husband goes off to work for 10 hours. I wish I could escape, too!"

- Sometimes parents feel angry at their deaf or hard of hearing child, then feel guilty about having that feeling. They may be angry that their "normal" life has been turned upside down. Appointments and added responsibilities now fill their days. They wonder if life will ever be the same.

Frustration

"Even though other family members and friends try to do as much as possible, I feel as if no one really understands our situation."

Disappointment:

- Some parents report feeling disappointed with family members and friends who either don't call and show support, or who don't know how to react and so neglect to say anything at all.

Guilt and Self-Reproach

- Hearing parents and hard of hearing parents often feel guilty when they realize they may have passed a hearing loss on to their child. (As mentioned earlier, many deaf parents are pleased to find out that their child is also deaf. In this case, they are less likely to experience guilt.)

- During the first few months following diagnosis, hearing parents may feel consumed by the need to find out why their child is deaf or hard of hearing.

"I kept wondering if I had done something wrong. Was it because I continued jogging through my eighth month? Was it the lighter fluid my husband used on the barbeque when we went camping?"

Anxiety

- This can range from a slight sense of insecurity to more intense and persistent feelings of panic. Here is how some parents reported feeling —

  *"For weeks I stayed up until midnight reading every book I could get my hands on about deafness. I was a nervous wreck. I felt I had to **know everything, now!**"*

  "I kept wondering and worrying if I was doing enough for him. What if I'm making the wrong decision?"

  "We knew the first three years were critical for our child's development, and so we did everything all of the professionals told us to do. We felt the professionals knew best, and we no longer had the self-confidence to make decisions about what would work for our child and family."

  "I kept fearing he might lose the rest of his hearing."

  "I had a hard time sleeping. I kept getting stomach aches, and I felt so restless."

  "About a year after my daughter's diagnosis, I suddenly began experiencing shortness of breath and a tightness in my chest. After a thorough medical exam, my doctor decided these were a result of the stress and anxiety I was feeling."

Fatigue

- Parents often report feeling continually exhausted during the first few weeks or months after their child's diagnosis.

"I felt so tired. I was dragging myself to the appointments. It was a real accomplishment just to get the laundry and grocery shopping done. I didn't know where I could get the energy necessary for helping my child."

Helplessness

- Parents report feeling incapable of helping their child.

"My minister told me that God had selected me to be Mathew's mother, because he knew I could handle it. I disagreed. I felt God had made a terrible mistake. He picked the wrong mother. I didn't think I would be able to do anything to help my child."

"I felt unable to do simple things, like writing a cheque in my chequebook."

Shock

- Parents report feeling numb, feeling as if nothing is real.

"I heard what they were saying to me, but I had no reaction. I felt as though I was standing outside my own body, uninvolved with the situation."

Yearning

- Parents may experience feelings of yearning for the normal hearing child they had (or thought they had). Parents also long for the normal life they had before the diagnosis. (No appointments then with doctors, audiologists, teachers, therapists, sign language instructors.)

Relief

- Parents who've had to fight their way through a maze of doctors who tell them everything is okay with their child may experience relief when they finally have a diagnosis.

  *"After all those months of worrying, I finally knew what was wrong. I could get on with the business of helping Scott, now that I had a diagnosis. I felt relief. I was **not** crazy. My son's hearing loss was not my imagination."*

STEPS TO TAKE IN ADAPTING TO LOSS

Grieving is the process of adapting to loss. There are four tasks to this adaptation process. For grieving to be complete, an individual must work through these four tasks. These common feelings may happen at different times for different people; they do not always occur in the same time sequence for everyone. For instance, a parent may be learning to adjust to the new reality (task 3) but may still experience times when they feel the pain of their grief (task 2).

Sometimes parents get stuck in one part of this process or do not complete the grieving experience. Incomplete grieving can stop parents from moving forward in their lives. Many parents benefit from meeting with a registered family counsellor or psychologist during this difficult time in their lives.

Task One: Accepting the Reality of the Loss

Parents must come full face with reality: their child is deaf or hard of hearing, and medicine will not cure him. Here are some of the experiences reported by parents as they were coming to terms with the reality of their child's hearing loss.

Searching For a Sign That Their Child Is Not Deaf or Searching For a Cure

- Parents report banging pots and pans near a child's ears to see if he or she will respond to sound. Sometimes parents search for other reasons that might explain the diagnosis. For instance: the child was not paying attention during testing, or the audiologist did not have experience testing young children.

Denying the Facts

- Some parents may ignore the truth of the audiologist's report.

  "Maybe the hearing loss is not as bad as the audiologist reported. She will grow out of it."

  Thinking in this way may protect the parent from feeling the full intensity of loss; but if this continues for a long time, it will slow the parent's progress towards accepting reality.

Denying the Significance of the Hearing Loss

- Parents may believe that hearing aids will "solve all problems." Or that their child will develop normally without any additional support, assistance, or information provided for the child or family.

Putting Emotions Aside For the Time Being While Doing What Needs to Be Done Immediately

- Many parents recognize the urgency with which they need to respond to change the situation where their child has limited or no access to language. In order to get information, make decisions, go to appointments, and advocate for their child, many parents describe how they cope with the pain of loss by making sure that they are doing what needs to be done for their child. For example, one parent recalled how getting a cochlear implant for her child as quickly as possible, even though it meant offending some people, helped her survive the pain she felt for her child, although it didn't make the pain go away altogether.

Denying That the Hearing Loss Is Irreversible

- Parents may continue hoping for a cure.

"If they can put a man on the moon, certainly they can find a cure for deafness."

If parents get stuck in the task of accepting the reality and permanence of their child's hearing loss, their denial may prevent them from taking important action — like learning sign language or putting hearing aids or a cochlear implant on a child.

Feeling Anger at the Professionals Who Bring the News of the Hearing Loss And Force the Parent to Face Reality

Task Two: Experiencing the Pain of Grief

If parents do not allow themselves to feel the pain of grief, the mourning process may last longer. Here are several examples:

Some Parents Fear That If They Give In To Experiencing Pain, Their Lives May Fall Apart

- They fear they will be unable to cope, so they try to avoid feeling anything. One spouse may try to find relief from these emotions through drinking or overeating. Another may immerse himself in his job to avoid any feeling. These parents are, of course, trying to cut off feelings-to deny the pain is real. Some parents may feel their child's situation is urgent and so will put aside their own feelings of grief to get done what needs to be done. Once they feel the habilitation process is under control, these parents may then allow themselves to begin grieving.

Some Report Crying for Days at a Time

- One mother says she sat at her kitchen table for two weeks, crying. Another told us she thought she was doing fine until one day in a shopping mall when she "just broke down" and realized there were tears running down her cheeks.

Occasionally, Friends Or Relatives Try to Stop Or Short-Circuit This Task of Experiencing the Pain of Grief

- They may try to reassure the parent and to stop the parent from crying. This is not helpful.

Those Who Grew Up in a Family Where Feelings Were Not Easily Expressed May Find It Difficult to Allow Themselves to Grieve

Sometimes, Parents Do Not Experience Pain at the Time of Diagnosis

- Instead, pain may come at a time of transition. For example, some parents told us that they believed initially that if they worked hard enough at talking with their child (the oral or auditory-verbal approach), the child would "become normal." These parents say they did not really experience grieving early on, because they wouldn't allow themselves to see the loss of the "hearing child." They had been convinced that, with their hard work, they would still have a hearing child. However, at the time they began considering the use of sign language, they were forced to face reality. At that point they started experiencing grief.

Parents Need to Work Through This Process of Experiencing the Pain of Grief So That They Do Not Carry the Pain With Them Forever

- Most parents continue to feel some sadness at times, but the feelings of sadness are usually less intense and occur less frequently as time passes. A few parents, however, do continue to feel a deep sadness throughout their lives.

Task Three: Adjusting to a New Reality

Parents Begin to Come to Terms With the Fact That Their Child May Need Hearing Aids Or a Cochlear Implant — Or May Need to Communicate in a Different Way Or Need Other Support

- They begin to adjust to the fact that they cannot call to their child from another part of the house and expect the child to respond. Some parents may also begin to adjust to the fact that their child may need to attend a specialized school or class, or that he may require additional therapy or an interpreter if he attends a regular class.

Some Parents May Try to Avoid This Task by Withdrawing

- They may begin avoiding their appointments with the audiologist, speech and language pathologist, or teacher. Occasionally parents fear that adjusting to the new reality means they have "given up" on their dream of having their child hear. These parents can become stuck or suspended at this point in the process and find it difficult to move forward.

Many Parents Begin a Quest For Information Related To Their Child's Hearing Loss

- They find it helpful to get information from a variety of sources and to obtain second opinions.

Parents may spend hours searching the internet and reading in the library. They can learn valuable information from other parents they meet at "Chat-Groups" as well as in support groups. Often parents find their anxiety decreases and a feeling of control over their lives returns as they gain more information about hearing loss, hearing devices, and communication.

When Parents Are Attempting to Adjust to the New Reality, Some May Start to See Their Situation From a Different Perspective: They May Look at the Positives

- For example, some parents say they had good feelings about learning new skills, meeting and becoming good friends with new people (other parents of deaf or hard of hearing children as well as deaf or hard of hearing adults) and finding out about a whole new world.

"I found it so helpful to make friends with other families who have deaf and hard of hearing children. I really felt they understood our life."

"During those first few years we were desperately trying to do everything possible to help our deaf son. This meant that our family life really was 'out of whack.' I have almost no memories of my hearing daughter from that time, because we were always so focused on the needs and progress of our deaf son. I now see that our hearing daughter also needed our attention and praise during those early years. I wish I'd known then that our son would truly turn out okay. If I had been more relaxed about everything, our family life would have been much better balanced."

Task Four: Taking the Emotional Energy They Had for the Hearing Child and Reinvesting It in Their Deaf or Hard of Hearing Child

- Parents begin to "let go" of their dreams of the "perfect" hearing child and slowly accept the child for who he is. One parent remembers when she first realized she was going through this process:

  "I finally realized, when I looked at Erik, I saw a child first. He also happened to be deaf. The deafness was now a part of who he was, and I loved this person."

- Parents often start searching for opportunities to be with other deaf or hard of hearing individuals in order to learn more about what their child's life might be like in the future. Whatever that future is, they know they want to be part of it.

WHEN IS GRIEVING FINISHED?

Grieving is completed when the tasks of grieving are over. How long this takes will vary from person to person.

- At this point, many parents begin to think of their child and the hearing loss without pain — without a physical response like crying or feeling an intense tightness in the chest. These parents feel they have returned to the business of living.

- But some parents have told us their grief never totally disappeared. Although they no longer felt sad most of the time, these feelings of sadness did return occasionally throughout the years.

- Transition times often bring about painful feelings. Parents may again experience sadness or longing at specific times. For instance: when their child moves on from preschool to elementary school, when their child marries, or when their child becomes a parent.

GETTING HELP

If you are experiencing some of the feelings described earlier in this chapter, you may benefit from getting some additional support. Many parents tell us they found it helpful to talk with other parents who had gone through a similar experience. The BC Family Hearing Resource Centre holds parent support group meetings to provide parents with a safe and comfortable place where they can share their concerns, sadness, frustrations and joy with others who can really understand.

If you live in a smaller community, you may not be aware of other families with deaf or hard of hearing children. Ask your audiologist if he knows of any similar families you might be able to contact. If you live in British Columbia, our Parent-to-Parent Support Network can also help connect you with other individual families or support groups.

For more information on the BCFHRC Parent-to-Parent Support Network,

     call: 604-584-2827 (voice)
              1-877-584-2827 (Toll Free)
              604-584-9108 (TTY)

  or write: BCFHRC Parent-to-Parent Support Network
              15220 92nd Avenue
              Surrey, British Columbia
              V3R 2T8

We also connect parents through our website at www.bcfamilyhearing.com. If you live in the United States you can contact the Hands and Voices organization to talk to other parents.

Web: www.handsandvoices.org
Toll free phone: 866-422-0422

What If Grieving Is Prolonged and Seriously Interferes With Your Life?

Sometimes parents need additional support from a trained family counsellor or psychologist. You can find out what counselling services are available in your community by contacting —

- A public health nurse

- Your family physician

- Yellow Pages: Look for associations of registered psychologists or family counsellors

- In British Columbia you can contact the Well-Being program for free counselling services.

Phone: 604-732-7656 (voice)
604-732-7549 (TTY
Web: www.vch.ca/wpb

CHAPTER 2

MAKING INITIAL DECISIONS

Making Decisions 17
What Research Does and Does Not Tell Us 22
What to Consider When Making Decisions About
    Communication 23
Family Communication Self-Evaluation 25

MAKING DECISIONS

Families with deaf and hard of hearing children face many difficult decisions. Parents may need to make a decision about a communication method, or whether to consider a cochlear implant for their child. Parents often report that they are terrified of making "critical, life-long" decisions for their children.

Gathering Information

Today, parents are fortunate to have easier access to vital information about hearing loss, hearing devices, communication, and habilitation. In Appendix A — Helpful Resources, you will find a wide variety of informational books, videos, and journals as well as lists of websites and professional and parent organizations. Take the time to gather the information you need in order to make decisions about your child.

Some parents have told us that they thought they would remember articles they had read, or telephone conversations they'd had with professionals or other parents, but later found it difficult to recall vital information. Start a journal or a notebook where you can record the date and the highlights of the information you read. Also, keep track of conversations and telephone calls in your journal.

You may find it confusing to be faced with conflicting opinions about a variety of relevant issues. Some professionals, as well as deaf and hard of hearing adults, may be quite passionate about their viewpoints. Not all professionals will agree, nor will all deaf or hard of hearing adults agree. Their opinions are often directly influenced by their own unique experiences. Keep reading and talking with other parents, professionals, and deaf and hard of hearing adults until you feel you have enough information to proceed.

Among the various professionals and service providers involved who may offer opinions about communication options, it is essential to have a communication specialist — with expertise in communication delays and disorders — who is able to assess your child's communication and provide information based on developmental norms. The following is a list of just a few of the communication specialists and service providers who can give you information about communication options. The descriptions are general and are meant to give you an idea of their education specialty and the role they will play in early intervention for your child. BC Family Hearing Resource Centre's professionals — speech-language pathologists and teachers of the deaf and hard of hearing — work together with families as a team. They involve other professionals, as well as service providers, to ensure appropriate, quality services.

Speech-Language Pathologist (S-LP)

In Canada and the United States, speech-language pathologists (S-LPs) usually have advanced graduate university degrees in communication. The Canadian Association of Speech Language Pathologists and Audiologists (CASLPA) and the American Speech-

> ## HANDLING CONFLICTING INFORMATION
>
> *"One of the most important foundations for parents to understand at the beginning of the journey, is that the information that they will be receiving from doctors, teachers, therapists, adults who are deaf/hard of hearing and other parents may be 'fact' based OR 'opinion' based. Often this information is delivered as factual information, when in reality it is the opinion of the person presenting it. Parents of newly identified children have a tool in their arsenal for decision making when they understand they can take all information given to them, and tease out what might be true for their own situation, and what might not actually be applicable for their own child and family."*
>
> *— Janet DesGeorges*
> *Outreach Director,*
> *Hands & Voices*

Language and Hearing Association (ASHA) grant certification to speech-language pathologists and audiologists who have a minimum of a Master's degree, have successfully completed a certification exam, and have successfully completed many hours of supervised practicums in a variety of settings. CASLPA and ASHA members are also required to continue updating their knowledge through continuing education. The role of the S-LP is to identify and assess communication disorders — also, to treat and manage these disorders once they are identified. Their work with children covers the areas of speech, voice and fluency — as well as cognitive (mental) processes necessary for communication.

Speech-language pathologists may or may not have had extensive experience with children with hearing loss. Your S-LP may use an auditory-verbal therapy approach even though she may or may not be certified as an Auditory-Verbal therapist (A-VT). An S-LP may be proficient with sign language or may know just a few signs, depending on experience and additional training. The BC Family Hearing Resource Centre provides advanced professional training for speech-language pathologists to gain additional expertise related to habilitation services for deaf and hard of hearing children and their families.

Teachers of the Deaf and Hard of Hearing (TDHH)

Teachers of the deaf and hard of hearing, also called Educators of the deaf and hard of hearing, may be referred to in mainstream schools as itinerant teachers of the deaf and hard of hearing or hearing resource teachers.

Teachers of the deaf and hard of hearing have teaching degrees and additional specialized education for working with children with hearing loss. Certification as a teacher of the deaf and hard of hearing requires additional study and experience in addition to a teaching degree. Some educators of the deaf have advanced graduate degrees. These educators will have received information about communication development, information about the psychological and social aspects of deafness, curriculum development for the classroom, and evaluation and instruction of deaf and hard of hearing children.

Teachers of the deaf and hard of hearing may or may not have received training in early intervention and family-centered care. The role of the teacher of the deaf and hard of hearing varies. With young children they may assess communication abilities and offer therapeutic strategies to facilitate listening, speech, and language development — as well as provide an appropriate, specialized educational curriculum. A TDHH may use an auditory-verbal approach to listening and communication development and may or may not have experience with sign language.

Certified Auditory-Verbal (A-VT) Therapist

Auditory-Verbal International, Inc® (AVI) is a private, non-profit international membership organization whose principal objective is to promote listening and speaking as a way of life for children who are deaf or hard of hearing. The auditory-verbal approach is a specific method developed to be used with children who are deaf or hard of hearing. However, many of the individual strategies used by Auditory-Verbal therapists have also been used in other therapeutic methods and approaches. The certified auditory-verbal therapist has accrued a minimum number of hours, under supervision, practicing the auditory-verbal methods with the deaf and hard of hearing.

From a parent:

"As we were struggling with the decisions, we spoke with several families who had had a range of successes with their children's implants. One was a young person who was flourishing with her new implant — now listening to her Walkman and learning to speak French. The other was a thriving snowboarding, teenage girl who didn't use her implant anymore and relied solely on signing."

"We asked ourselves (again and again) how would we feel if the implant failed? Our answer was always the same — at least we would have tried. We weren't prepared to delay the implant, then to look back in 5, 10, or 30 years and wonder whether our son had missed his only chance to hear."

Sign Language Instructor

A sign language instructor has expertise in using a visual language system (usually ASL) and has experience in instructing others — usually adults — in learning sign language. A sign language instructor is not required to have training in evaluating the communication of children with hearing loss, or in making recommendations about communication goals and strategies for children with hearing loss.

Refer to Chapter 23 for more information about how to be an advocate for your child with communication specialists and community service providers. The Appendix provides resources and links to information about various team members who may be involved with your child — as well as information regarding related professions. Other team members (for instance, Infant Development Consultants and Early Childhood Educators) are a part of the communication team that provides services to families.

Considering a Cochlear Implant for Your Child

If you are considering a cochlear implant for your child, you should be aware that current research indicates that **early** implantation can make a difference. Some parents are concerned about making such an important decision for their child and wish they could wait until their child is old enough to make this decision for himself. But that may be too late. Researchers are finding that, in general, the younger a child is, the more likely he is to benefit significantly from a cochlear implant.

It is important to talk to parents who have chosen a cochlear implant for their child. Talk, also, with parents who have decided against an implant. Talk to older children and teenagers who are successful users of the implant, as well as those who no longer use it.

Considering Sign Language for Your Child

Decisions about communication mode are not irreversible. We encourage families to remain open-minded and flexible. Families should make decisions about communication based on their observations of the needs of their child and family. These needs often change over time. We have seen families who started with speech and sign language and later changed to using only speech as their child's strengths and preferences became more obvious. We have seen other families who started with oral only, and then added sign language when they realized their child was not making enough progress.

Generally, the more delayed your child's communication abilities, the more likely she will benefit from the use of signs.

WHAT RESEARCH DOES AND DOES NOT TELL US

If you look through scientific journals to try to determine what is the best communication method, you might soon find yourself feeling confused. You would likely see the same number of research articles supporting an auditory-verbal approach as those that support sign language.

Scientific articles that are published in the Volta Review, a journal of the Alexander Graham Bell Association, usually support methods that promote oral communication. Whereas research articles that appear in the American Annals of the Deaf are often in support of sign language.

Educators may tell you that **their** method (Auditory-Oral, Auditory-Verbal, Cued Speech, ASL, Sign-Supported Speech, etc) is **best** for deaf and hard of hearing children. You should keep in mind that no **one** method has been scientifically proven to be best for **all** deaf or hard of hearing children. Your job will be to discover, over time, the best method of communication for your child and family.

What research **does** tell us is that good, early communication is related to the development of positive self-esteem and to later language-learning abilities. Research consistently shows that early language stimulation in **some mode** during a child's first two or three years of life is critical.

Therefore, if your child is making good progress using speech and listening, your family should feel confident in your decision to continue using an Auditory-Oral or Auditory-Verbal approach. However, you might need to consider changing your decision if —

- Your child has only gained a few new words in the past three to six months.

- Your child is very frustrated.

- Your family does not understand your child's communication much of the time.

- Your child is missing lots of learning opportunities; because, much of the time he does not discriminate speech well enough to understand what is said around him.

- Your child has additional challenges and may learn more easily with a multi-sensory communication approach (e.g., picture symbols, sign-supported speech).

WHAT TO CONSIDER WHEN MAKING DECISIONS ABOUT COMMUNICATION

When families are concerned about communication modes, we encourage them to monitor their child's progress

— together with a communication specialist — and to re-evaluate decisions about choice of communication every three to six months. Use the **Family Communication Self-Evaluation** on the next page to help you evaluate your decision.

FAMILY COMMUNICATION SELF-EVALUATION

Note: Your speech-language pathologist, educator of the deaf and hard of hearing, and other specialists use formal and informal assessments to record speech, listening, and language abilities on a timely basis. Your observations and participation in these evaluations help to measure your baby's progress over time. Formal assessments are tests that compare your child's skills to other children of the same age. Informal assessments are checklists and language samples that are for your own use.

Am I continuing to use a communication method because of what I have been **promised** will happen or because of what I have **observed** in my child?

How much progress has my child made in the area of communication over the last three to six months? How does this compare to gains made by a hearing child of the same age?

How does my child try to communicate with me most of the time?

___ Is my child using speech more often than before?

___ Is my child using gestures more often than speech?

___ Is my child using signs more often than before?

___ When I am communicating with my baby, does he seem to pay attention and stay interested in what I am saying?

___ Does my child understand most of what I say when I am not adding gestures?

___ Does my child have access to the same information as other children do?

___ Do I enjoy communicating with my child, or is it usually a frustrating experience?

___ Can we communicate easily enough so that I am able to talk with my child about what is happening?

___ Does my child seem to be developing a sense of self-confidence?

___ Does my child feel successful in communicating with others in his life?

___ Is my child frustrated when communicating — withdrawing and showing an increase in tantrums?

___ Do I frequently find myself using gestures in order to help my child understand what I mean?

CHAPTER 3

COMMON CAUSES AND TYPES OF HEARING LOSS

Common Causes of Hearing Loss 27
Other Causes of Hearing Loss 28
Types of Hearing Loss 29

COMMON CAUSES OF HEARING LOSS

One of the first questions parents ask when their baby is diagnosed with a hearing loss is: "What caused my child's hearing loss?" Some hearing loss is caused by genetics and some is caused by a medical condition. Sometimes the cause of a child's hearing loss remains unknown. Listed below are medical conditions or events that are known to be sometimes associated with a hearing loss; these are known as risk factors:

- Family history of childhood hearing loss

- Infection during pregnancy (rubella, cytomegalovirus/CMV, syphilis, herpes, or toxoplasmosis)

- Anomalies of the head and neck (e.g. malformed outer ear)

- Low birth weight (under 3.3 pounds)

- Hyperbilirubinemia (jaundice)

- Bacterial meningitis

- Ototoxic medications (medications that can damage hearing)

- Mechanical ventilation (respirator) for more than five days

- Deprivation of oxygen at birth

OTHER CAUSES OF HEARING LOSS

Babies are sometimes born with other related symptoms in addition to their hearing loss. There are over three hundred syndromes that have hearing loss as one of the symptoms. Researchers at Boys Town National Research Hospital in Nebraska have listed **the ten most common syndromes** associated with hearing loss as being:

1. Hemifacial microsomia
2. Stickler syndrome
3. Congenital cytomegalovirus
4. Usher syndrome
5. Branchio-oto-renal syndrome
6. Pendred syndrome
7. CHARGE Association
8. Neurofibromatosis type II
9. Mitochondrial disorders
10. Waardenburg syndrome

Research studies suggest that about one-third of all children with hearing loss have one or more additional special needs. These can include visual, physical, or other special conditions. If you have questions about the cause of your child's hearing loss or are concerned about the possibility of your child having additional special needs, you can ask your doctor to help arrange for a comprehensive assessment (including vision) and genetic evaluation.

TYPES OF HEARING LOSS

If your child has been diagnosed with a permanent hearing loss, the specialists may have told you the name for your child's type of hearing loss. To help you better understand your child's hearing loss we have briefly described here some **types** of hearing loss. Types of hearing loss can be described in terms of **where** the hearing loss occurs in the ear, and **how long** the hearing loss has been there.

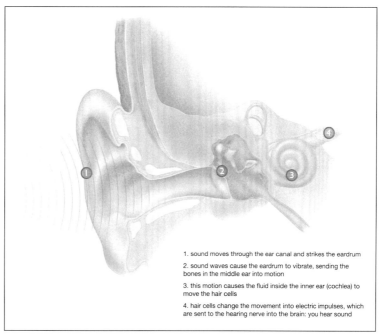

1. sound moves through the ear canal and strikes the eardrum

2. sound waves cause the eardrum to vibrate, sending the bones in the middle ear into motion

3. this motion causes the fluid inside the inner ear (cochlea) to move the hair cells

4. hair cells change the movement into electric impulses, which are sent to the hearing nerve into the brain: you hear sound

How hearing works.

Reprinted with permission from Cochlear Canada Inc.

Conductive Hearing Loss

The term "conductive" hearing loss means something is wrong with the **external** part of the ear or with the **middle** ear. For instance, a child's external ear canal might be absent or incomplete, or there might be something wrong with the three little bones in the middle ear, or the middle ear might be filled with fluid. In conductive hearing loss, sound is not conducted properly to the inner ear. Sometimes a conductive loss is considered to be **temporary** when it is a type of problem that can be medically treated (such as fluid in the middle ear). A child with a **permanent** conductive hearing loss may benefit from a bone-conduction aid or a bone-anchored hearing aid.

Sensorineural Hearing Loss

The term "sensorineural" hearing loss means something is wrong with the **inner ear** (the cochlea or auditory nerve). This is a permanent type of hearing loss. Although the cause of a sensorineural hearing loss is often unknown, common causes in young children can include lack of oxygen during birth, pre-natal infections, and genetics (passed through the family). Depending on the **degree** of hearing loss, children with a sensorineural hearing loss may have difficulty understanding speech. Most children with a sensorineural hearing loss will benefit from a hearing device such as a hearing aid or a cochlear implant.

Mixed Hearing Loss

The term "mixed" hearing loss means a child has both a sensorineural hearing loss and a conductive hearing loss. For instance, some children with a **permanent** sensorineural hearing loss also develop **temporary** middle ear problems, such as fluid in the middle ear. Parents should seek medical attention for **any** temporary middle ear problems, because these can result in the child having increased difficulty hearing sound and understanding speech. Parents of children with permanent sensorineural hearing losses will want to limit the amount of time their child's hearing is made even worse by the added complication of temporary middle-ear problems. Young children who are still learning language need every hearing opportunity they can get.

Auditory Neuropathy and Auditory Dysynchrony (AN and AD)

The child's external, middle, and inner ear or cochlea seem to receive sounds normally; but the child still has a hearing loss. In auditory neuropathy and dysynchrony (AN and AD) there is a problem somewhere along the auditory nerve from the nerve contacting the hair cells to the auditory centers in the brain system.

Often a child with AN or AD has more difficulty understanding speech than would be expected from the level of that child's hearing loss, and he or she may have more difficulty hearing in noisy situations. A child's response to sound may fluctuate (change) over time. Some children with AN or AD benefit from hearing aids, though many do not. Some children benefit from a cochlear implant and some do not. No one yet knows the cause of auditory neuropathy or dysynchrony, but children who experienced problems at birth or who were born prematurely seem to have a higher risk for AN and AD.

Unilateral Hearing Loss

The child has a hearing loss in only one ear. A unilateral hearing loss can be conductive, sensorineural, or mixed (both conductive and sensorineural). Most children with unilateral hearing loss will hear adequately in **ideal** listening situations but may have significant problems understanding speech when there is background noise — or when speech is directed towards the child's ear that has a hearing loss. People sometimes underestimate the potential effect a unilateral hearing loss can have on a child's speech and language development. Parents can help prevent problems by following the suggestions in this book related to reducing background noise, as well as ideas for promoting a child's speech and language development.

Congenital Hearing Loss

Hearing loss is present at birth.

Acquired Hearing Loss

A hearing loss that is the result of something else happening any time after birth; that is, there is a period of time when the child's hearing is normal before the hearing loss occurs. Hearing loss from Meningitis and Noise-Induced Hearing Loss are examples of acquired hearing loss. An acquired hearing loss is typically sensorineural, but may be mixed or conductive as well.

Progressive Hearing Loss

A child has a progressive hearing loss when his hearing loss gets worse over time. This type of hearing loss tends to be sensorineural.

Delayed Onset Hearing Loss

A child appears to have been born with normal hearing and later develops a hearing loss. This type of hearing loss tends to be sensorineural. It may also be described as **pre- or post-lingual** (before or after the child acquired spoken language).

CHAPTER 4

HEARING TESTS AND RESULTS: WORKING TOGETHER WITH YOUR PEDIATRIC AUDIOLOGIST

*What Hearing Tests Are Used With Babies
     and Children? 33*
Understanding Audiograms 35
Working With My Audiologist 44
Questions for My Audiologist 46

WHAT HEARING TESTS ARE USED WITH BABIES AND CHILDREN?

Audiologists may use a few different hearing tests to evaluate your child's hearing. The audiologist will usually compare the results of the various tests to determine if your child has a hearing loss. If your child does have a hearing loss, then the audiologist will also use the test results to determine the **type** and **amount** of hearing loss. These results will provide information the audiologist needs in order to make hearing device recommendations and fine-tune the hearing aids.

Hearing Tests for Newborn Babies

There are two types of hearing tests that are used to test newborn babies for hearing loss — **auditory brainstem response** and **otoacoustic emissions.** These tests can also be used with older babies and children.

- **Auditory Brainstem Response (ABR):** Sensors (electrodes) are placed on the child's scalp. Sounds are presented to each ear through insert phone tips or headphones while the child is sleeping or is sedated. The child's auditory nerve and brainstem responses to different pitches and loudness levels of sound are monitored and recorded. This test can give hearing thresholds. When the ABR test is automated for screening it is called Automated Auditory Brain Stem Response (AABR)

- **Otoacoustic Emissions (OAE):** The audiologist puts a soft plug with a sensitive microphone in the child's ear canal. The audiologist plays several "clicks" or "tones." If the child's cochlear hair cells are normal, a response is found. If there is no response, the child may have a hearing loss and will be referred on for further testing.

Hearing Tests for Children

Here are some additional hearing tests and procedures that may be used with young children. These tests help to determine the **amount** and / or **type** of hearing loss.

- **Impedance Testing (tympanometry):** A small probe is placed in the child's ear while the movement of the eardrum is measured. This test shows if there is a problem in the middle ear, such as middle-ear fluid, which may precede, accompany, or follow a middle-ear infection.

- **Visual Reinforced Audiometry:** The audiologist presents sounds to a child or an infant seated on an adult's lap or being held by an adult, through speakers or headphones. A toy lights up or moves (for instance a clown lights up and dances) as soon as a child indicates in some way that he is aware of the sound that has been presented. The child learns that when he looks towards the sound he is then rewarded or reinforced with the moving or "lit-up" toy. This testing interprets the child's bahaviour, and is sometimes referred to as "bahavioural testing."

- **Play Audiometry** or **Conditioned Play Audiometry(CPA):** The audiologist presents sounds to a child through speakers or headphones. The child is taught to respond to the sounds by performing an action (for instance, putting a block in a bucket or a peg in a pegboard) immediately after he detects a sound. CPA is also a form of bahavioural testing.

UNDERSTANDING AUDIOGRAMS

Audiologists will often record the results of Visual Reinforced Audiometry and Conditioned Play Audiometry tests on an audiogram. Audiograms are one piece of information that tells you something about your child's hearing.

Audiograms are not always easy to understand. The next few pages will help you to better understand your child's audiogram.

An **audiogram** is used by an audiologist to graph how well your child can hear in a sound-proof booth. Tones are presented to your child, either through headphones or through speakers, at different loudness levels. Depending on the age of your child, he may indicate he has heard a tone by raising his hand, dropping a block, or simply turning his head. When the audiologist is confident that the response is true, he records a symbol on the audiogram. Generally, the audiologist will continue to present many low- and high-pitch tones to your child. For each tone, the symbol she records will represent the quietest sound level — where your child shows that he can just barely hear the tone. This is his **hearing threshold for that tone.**

A tone is a **frequency** (think of pitch), and it is measured in **Hertz** (Hz). A very low tone or frequency would be 250 Hz, and a higher tone would be 4000 Hz. Intensity (think of loudness) on the other hand, is measured in decibels (dB). Quiet tones would be 0-20 dB, comfortable tones would be 30-60 dB, and loud tones would be 70 dB and above.

Most **speech tones** occur naturally within the region of the banana-like shape in the middle of the audiogram. This shape is sometimes called the "speech banana." Speech sounds will occur within this region when spoken at a normal loudness for conversation (around 50 dB). In order to easily understand speech sounds spoken at normal conversation level, sound detection (the softest level where you just barely hear a sound) must be at least 20-30 dB better than the loudness level of conversation.

With your audiologist, speech-language pathologist, or teacher of the deaf and hard of hearing, try copying the results of your child's audiogram onto the sample audiogram. Notice where your child's hearing thresholds are graphed. If some thresholds are above the speech banana (**a slight-to-mild hearing loss**), your child can hear the speech sounds that occur directly below — although he may need to pay greater attention to them, and they may be unclear or "fuzzy".

If some thresholds are within or just below the speech banana (**a moderate-to-moderately-severe hearing loss**), your child will have more difficulty hearing the speech sounds in that area. He will be able to perceive some speech tones, but they are likely to be quieter and distorted. Speech sounds are more likely to sound similar and less distinct from one another.

If your child's thresholds are well below the range of the speech banana (**a severe-to-profound hearing loss**), he will not hear speech tones at a normal level without the benefit of hearing aids or a cochlear implant.

Although most children can make use of hearing aids to discriminate speech sounds or to be aware of some differences in speech sounds, there are some who cannot and may not benefit from conventional hearing aids. After an initial hearing aid trial, cochlear implantation may be recommended.

Of course, each child is unique. Sometimes a child's right ear will hear better than the left ear (or vice versa); or a child may hear some tones at quieter levels than others, as in the case of a child with a **sloping hearing loss.** This affects not only the overall loudness of a conversation but also the clearness of the sound. For example, think of a radio that is slightly "off the station". The quality of the sound is distorted. By adjusting only the volume dial, the sounds will become louder but not much clearer. This is because the problem is with the frequency or the pitch of the signal.

Your child's audiologist must, therefore, look at each audiogram in a unique way in order to recommend a hearing aid. Hearing aids can be fine-tuned to suit the needs of each child and his or her own type and degree of hearing loss.

Each frequency or pitch is looked at for possible volume gain. That is, how much gain is required at that frequency in order to allow the child to perceive the sound. Hearing aids can improve the loudness of a message. Unlike a radio, however, they cannot make speech tones perfectly clear. This is because of the damage to the hearing mechanism in the ear.

It will likely take several visits to the audiologist to determine the extent and type of hearing loss. Depending on the age and bahaviour of your child and the complexity of the hearing loss in terms of type and extent, the audiologist may not feel confident about the results — or get quite enough information — the first few tries.

Each visit is an opportunity to provide the audiologist with more information so that your child benefits from appropriate recommendations. In some cases, additional testing, using a bone conducting device, may be required if a conductive loss (middle ear) is suspected.

On the next few pages you will find examples of audiograms of children with various levels of hearing loss. The first audiogram shows normal hearing, followed by audiograms showing mild hearing loss, moderate hearing loss, sloping to severe, and severe hearing loss.

Symbols on an Audiogram

These symbols (**X, O, A,** and **S**) are recorded by the audiologist as a graphical representation of how well your child can perceive different sound frequencies

X = Hearing of the left ear without hearing aids, through headphones.

O = Hearing of the right ear without hearing aids, through headphones.

A = Hearing testing with hearing aids through speakers. Because both ears are being tested at the same time, the results show the aided hearing of the ear with the better hearing.

S = Hearing tested without hearing aids, through speakers rather than through head phones. Because both ears are being tested at the same time, the results show the unaided hearing of the better ear.

< = Bone conduction testing of the **left** ear. (See Bone Conduction Testing in the glossary section of Appendix D: Glossary.)

> = Bone conduction testing of the **right** ear.

Need help understanding the audiologist's report? See Appendix D: Glossary.

If you have further questions or concerns about audiograms, hearing testing, or your child's hearing loss, you can -

- Talk to a doctor (otologist).

- Talk to your audiologist (not once but many times) or to another audiologist.

- Talk to a speech-language pathologist, a teacher of the deaf and hard of hearing, or an auditory-verbal therapist.

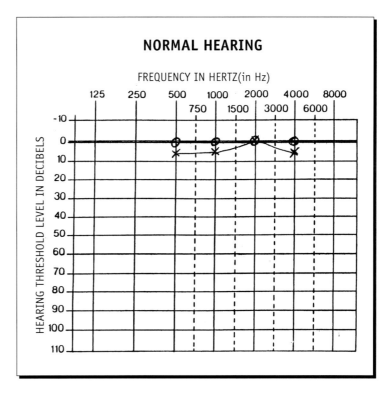

This an example of an audiogram for a child with normal hearing.

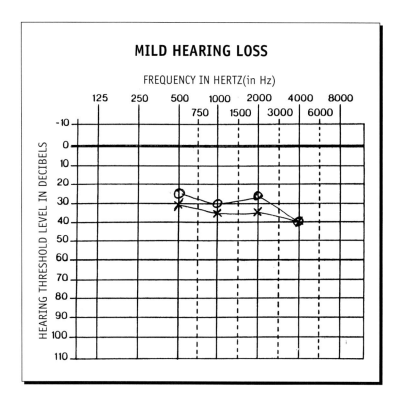

MILD HEARING LOSS

FREQUENCY IN HERTZ(in Hz)

This audiogram shows a mild hearing loss in both ears. Look across the top to see frequency and look down the left side to see the level of loudness. Look at the X symbol that is farthest to the left. It is sitting on the vertical line at 30 decibels (dB) and on the horizontal line at 500 Hertz (Hz).

This indicates that this child can just barely hear the low pitch tone of 500Hz from his left ear when it is presented at a loudness level of 30 dB.

Moving to the right, draw your finger from the first X at 500 Hz to the next X at 1000 Hz.

This second X indicates that the child can just barely hear from his left ear the 1000 Hz tone when it is presented at 35 dB. Now, move all the way to the right and find the last

X sitting on the vertical line of 4000 Hz and the horizontal line of 40 dB.

This indicates that the child can just barely hear the high pitch tone of 4000 Hz. when it is presented at a loudness level of 40 dB.

Look back on the left side of the chart and find the O symbols. See if you can determine how well this child can hear with his right ear at 500 Hz, 1000 Hz, and 4000 Hz.

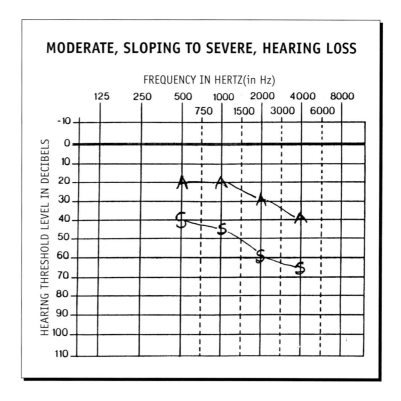

This audiogram shows a child with a moderate, sloping to severe, hearing loss. The child has a **moderate** hearing loss in the lower pitch tones, and his hearing loss is worse (**severe**) in the higher pitch tones.

The "**S**" symbols show that the child's hearing was tested through loud speakers rather than through ear phones. This means the audiologist does not yet know the test results for each individual ear, but she can say that the child's hearing from his best ear is at the level shown with the S.

The "**A**" symbols show how the child responded to sound while he was using hearing aids.

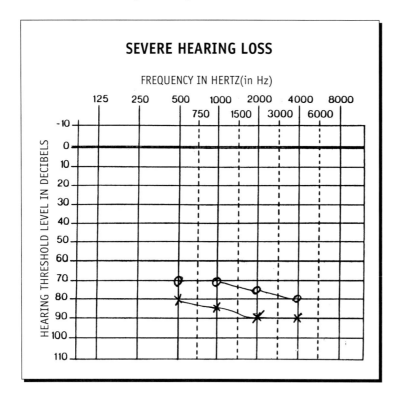

This audiogram of a child with a **severe** hearing loss is characterized by the graph showing the hearing threshold in both ears well below 60 dB.

SAMPLE AUDIOGRAM

Try copying the results of your child's hearing test onto this audiogram.

The "Speech Banana" shows those sounds heard in normal conversation such as **sh** in *shoe*, **ch** in *church*, **ng** in *sing*, **m** in *mom*, and **th** in *the*.

NAME OF CHILD: _____   DATE OF BIRTH: _____

DESCRIPTION OF HEARING LOSS: _____

_____

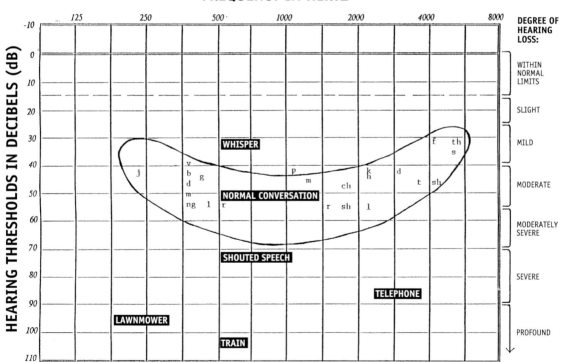

FREQUENCY IN HERTZ

BC Family Hearing Resource Centre

Bright futures for Children

KEY: AIR CONDUCTION
 A — Aided
 O — Right Ear Unaided
 X — Left Ear Unaided

BONE CONDUCTION
 < Left Ear
 > Right Ear

WORKING WITH MY AUDIOLOGIST

Why Does the Audiologist Need My Observations?

- You can help the audiologist understand your child's responsiveness to sound when he is wearing hearing aids.

- After your child is fitted with hearing aids, the audiologist will probably want to see him on several occasions in order to test his aided hearing (what he is able to hear when wearing his hearing aids).

- You can help the audiologist by sharing your observations about your child. The audiologist is best able to evaluate your child's hearing aids — and the settings on these aids — when she combines information from the audiological testing, together with the observations of your child that you make. When you visit the audiologist, be sure to take along the chart that appears in Chapter 6 — Hearing Aid Use: My Personal Chart, page 78 .

*The audiologist and I can work together to assess
my child's hearing loss and hearing device use.*

What Information Does the Audiologist Need From Me?

• How your child responds to sound

• How your child uses his voice

• Problems or concerns about hearing aids

Questions For My Audiologist

When parents are first faced with the news that their baby
has a hearing loss, they sometimes find it difficult to listen
and to remember all of the new information they are given
by various specialists.

To help you keep track of the information you may need or
want to know, we've listed common topics and questions
on the following pages that are frequently asked by
parents. Take this with you the next time you visit your
audiologist.

QUESTIONS FOR MY AUDIOLOGIST

I want more information about:

HEARING AIDS

Hearing Devices:

___ Why was this particular hearing aid or cochlear implant recommended for my child?

___ How will the choice of this hearing device affect the use of FM later?

___ How long will my child's hearing aids or cochlear implant last?

Earmolds:

___ What are the advantages of different ear molds for my child?

___ How often will the ear molds need replacing and what will that cost?

___ What causes acoustic feedback and how can I prevent it?

Batteries:

___ What kind should I use?

___ Where can I buy batteries?

___ How do I check them?

___ If they are rechargeable-how do I recharge them?

___ How often will they need to be replaced, and what will that cost me?

___ What conditions will require more battery power?

Daily Check:

___ Why is it important for me to check the hearing device and batteries daily?

___ What is the best time of day to check the hearing device and batteries?

___ When I listen through the stethoscope or ear bud, am I hearing what my child hears with the hearing device?

What other equipment should I buy?

Hearing Aids:

___ Dry Aid Kit ___ Fishing Line ___ Stethoscope

___ Blower ___ Battery tester ___ Wig Tape

Other Questions:

___ Why should I buy insurance for this hearing device, and where can I buy it?

___ What are some practical hints for keeping the hearing device on?

___ Are there some deaf or hard of hearing children or adults who never use a hearing device?

QUESTIONS FOR MY AUDIOLOGIST (cont'd)

I want more information about:

AUDIOGRAMS

___ What do the symbols on the audiogram mean?

___ What severity or degree of loss does my child have?

___ How might this hearing loss affect his development (language / speech / learning)?

___ What do you think my child can hear with hearing aids?

___ What do you think my child can hear without hearing aids?

___ Now that my child has hearing aids, why is he not responding yet?

___ Why do the responses change? (Why does the audiologist get different result on different days?)

___ How did the audiologist know my child was able to — or not able to — hear certain sounds?

___ Since my child is not developmentally up to his chronological age (he has additional speech needs), how can the audiologist know accurately what my child can hear?

___ Are hearing tests the same for all ages? What kinds of tests are used at different ages?

___ What does ABR (Auditory Brainstem Response) testing tell you?

___ Can children learn how to trick audiologists so that the test results are wrong?

___ I want to be able to better understand the audiologist's written report.

___ My child responds to sound even without hearing aids on. Does he really need the aids?

QUESTIONS FOR MY AUDIOLOGIST (cont'd)

I want more information about:

COCHLEAR IMPLANTS

___ Who do I contact for more information about cochlear implants?

___ Is my child eligible for a cochlear implant?

___ Is there more than one type of cochlear implant?

___ What is the difference between an ear level and a body processor?

___ What does the research show about cochlear implant use?

___ What do I need to know about electrostatic discharge?

___ Under what conditions would the cochlear implant ever need to be surgically removed?

___ Are there some cochlear implant wearers (children or adults with surgically implanted devices) who never use the cochlear implant?

___ Can my child have two implants?

QUESTIONS FOR MY AUDIOLOGIST (cont'd)

I want more information about:

ASSISTIVE LISTENING DEVICES

___ Would assistive listening devices such as FM equipment help my child?

___ Do you recommend technical devices for the home (alerting devices, fire alarm system, telephone device for the deaf, closed caption for TV)?

___ Do Cochlear Implant users benefit from Assistive Listening Devices?

I would like more information about:

COMMUNICATION METHODS AND EDUCATIONAL APPROACHES

___ What is oral language, sign language, sign-supported speech and cued speech?

___ What is auditory-verbal therapy?

___ Can you recommend books or videotapes that describe different methods?

___ Can you arrange for me to meet oral or signing deaf or hard of hearing adults?

___ Can you arrange for me to meet other parents of deaf or hard of hearing children?

I would like more information about:

OTHER CONCERNS

___ Needs of siblings.

___ Behaviour management.

___ Tax benefits.

___ Financial assistance.

___ Transportation.

___ Organizations for deaf and hard of hearing individuals.

QUESTIONS FOR MY AUDIOLOGIST (cont'd)

I would like more information about:

COPING

___ BC Family Hearing Resource Centre Parent-to-Parent Support Network.

___ Books written by other parents.

___ Books written by professionals to help me cope with the fact that I am the parent of a deaf or hard of hearing child.

___ Books written by deaf or hard of hearing individuals about their experiences.

___ Videotapes of parents talking about their experiences.

___ Counselling services available.

___ Meeting with or phoning another parent of a hearing-impaired child.

CHAPTER 5

GETTING STARTED WITH HEARING AIDS

Why Should I Put Hearing Aids On My Child? 51
Will My Child's Response To Sound Change Immediately
  With Hearing Aids? 52
What If A Cochlear Implant Is Being Considered
  For My Child? 52
What If My Child Has Additional Special Needs? 53
How Do I Feel About Putting A Hearing Device
  On My Child? 54
Are All Hearing Aids the Same? 54
Which Type of Hearing Aid Is Best for My Child? 58
Earmolds 62
Getting Started With Hearing Aids 63
Keeping Hearing Aids On 66

WHY SHOULD I PUT HEARING AIDS ON MY CHILD?

Early, full-time use of a hearing device is strongly connected to speech and language development. If the first thing you do is to get hearing aids for your child, you will have begun to meet your child's needs by giving him the essential tools for learning to listen.

We know from recent research that there are critical times in a child's life when the auditory area of the brain is best equipped to develop. The first few years of a child's life are the most important years for learning to understand the sounds around him (including his parents' speech).

Auditory stimulation — or the input of sound — is critical for the formation of auditory pathways within the auditory area of your child's brain. Research shows that babies in the womb are able to receive sound from the outside world

From a parent:

"Sometimes parents are told to 'wait and see.' My son had a huge advantage because his hearing loss was diagnosed soon after birth, and he began wearing hearing aids by the time he was four months old. I urge other parents to do anything they can to get those hearing aids on immediately, so that their child can begin getting auditory input during this critical time of life."

and are probably already beginning to get ready to learn through listening. This is why we strongly encourage you to get information and support from professionals and from other parents, so that — as soon as possible — you can help your child begin using hearing aids throughout the day. Your child's listening skills will likely become more delayed the longer he is without appropriate hearing equipment.

If your child wears his hearing device for only a few minutes a day, the auditory area of his brain is getting only minimal stimulation. However, when your child begins wearing hearing aids or a cochlear implant for many hours a day, he'll be exposed to a great variety of sounds in his environment; and he will have many chances to learn from listening to your speech. When a cochlear implant is being considered, full-time hearing aid use may be required to determine eligibility as quickly as possible.

WILL MY CHILD'S RESPONSE TO SOUND CHANGE IMMEDIATELY WITH HEARING AIDS?

Hearing aids are designed to make sounds louder. Most children receive some benefit from this increase in loudness, but it is not always possible to predict from an audiogram how much a child will benefit from hearing aids or when he will begin showing a response to sound. It is important for the audiologist to measure what your child may hear with and without hearing equipment. This helps the audiologist fine-tune the equipment to meet your child's needs. It will also be important for you to observe your child's response to sound and his attempts to communicate. This will help the audiologist to evaluate your child's hearing aids.

From a parent:

"For the first many months I felt discouraged. I thought my child wasn't benefiting from hearing aids. I often wondered if it was worth all the effort. But, after a year, I started noticing changes in her response to sound: and she began trying to imitate some of our speech. Now, two years later, our daughter refuses to part with her hearing aids!"

From a parent:

"I wish someone had let me know that a small percentage of profoundly deaf children benefit very little from hearing aids — no matter how hard the parent tries."

WHAT IF A COCHLEAR IMPLANT IS BEING CONSIDERED FOR MY CHILD?

When a cochlear implant is being considered for your child, you will want to make sure your child wears his hearing aids full-time. This will help to determine, more quickly, which option is best for your child — a hearing aid or a cochlear implant.

When your child wears hearing aids or a cochlear implant, you are giving him the opportunity to learn to associate sounds with specific meanings. For instance, noise from the vacuum is associated with the machine Dad uses for cleaning, or the sound "Mama" becomes associated with the woman who is his mother.

WHAT IF MY CHILD HAS ADDITIONAL SPECIAL NEEDS?

Parents of children with multiple needs sometimes feel overwhelmed by all they must do. Their child may be ill frequently — or may require special help in many areas of his development. Because of this, parents may feel there are higher priorities in their child's life; and they may be tempted to put off the hearing aids until months later. It is important to know, though, that recent research has shown that children with multiple needs also benefit significantly from early hearing aid use. We now know that the critical period of auditory development in the brain that applies to all children applies to children with multiple needs as well. If your child has multiple needs you may require additional support from other parents or professionals in finding ways to successfully cope with hearing aids.

HOW DO I FEEL ABOUT PUTTING A HEARING DEVICE ON MY CHILD?

- When a deaf or hard of hearing child is born to hearing parents, most parents enter into a grieving process. Ongoing grieving can result as a response to the "death" of the dream of having a perfect baby.

- When parents are out in public with their child, they may find strangers staring or coming up to them to ask about the hearing aids or cochlear implant. Some parents report experiencing anger or embarrassment when this happens the first few times.

- Continuing to mourn over having a deaf or hard of hearing child may make it difficult for parents to put hearing aids on their child. When parents are struggling with their own emotions and are feeling apprehensive about hearing aids or a cochlear implant, it can seem like an insurmountable challenge to find ways to encourage their child to use the hearing device.

- What if you are experiencing these feelings? Talk with other parents who have already been through this with their child. Ask your audiologist to introduce you to some other families with similar problems. If you live in a more isolated area, you can contact us at the BC Family Hearing Resource Centre, and we'll put you in touch with other families who understand your experience.

ARE ALL HEARING AIDS THE SAME?

The majority of children with a hearing loss use **air conduction** hearing aids, which amplify sound into

From a parent:

"I think a parent's attitude can have a big impact on how a child feels about hearing aids. If the parent is feeling unhappy, uneasy, or anxious about putting the hearing aids on, the child will sense this emotion and react negatively, too."

From a parent:

"My first two children, who have severe hearing losses, responded immediately with their hearing aids. My third child, who has a profound loss, did not respond to sounds until one and a half years of hearing aid use. I didn't know if he would ever benefit from the hearing aids, but I'm glad I kept putting them on."

From a parent:

"I hated putting those hearing aids on during the first several months. The hearing aids were a constant and painful reminder to me that she had a hearing loss. That first Christmas I took her hearing aids off before any pictures were taken. It helped me a lot when I was able to talk with other parents."

a child's ear canal. But there are various types of air conduction hearing aids based on **style** (the hearing aid is worn either behind the ear or in the ear) and on the type of **electronics** used. **Bone conduction** hearing aids are another kind of hearing aid described at the end of this section. Different types of hearing aids that your audiologist might recommend for your child are briefly described on the next few pages. Based on your child's listening needs and the type and severity of hearing loss, your audiologist will recommend a device that best suits your child.

Air Conduction Hearing Aids

All air conduction hearing aids have similar components that include:

- A microphone to pick up sound

- An amplifier to make the sound louder

- Batteries to power the device

Hearing Aid Styles

- Behind-the-ear hearing aids: The parts of the hearing aid are contained in a small case which rests behind the ear and is connected by a tube to an ear mold in the child's ear.

- In-the-canal or in-the-ear hearing aids: In-the-ear hearing aids are so small they fit inside the ear canal or inside the outer part of the ear.

- Body-Aid: A microphone, amplifier, and battery are housed in a small unit which may be worn in a harness on the chest. This is then connected to the ear mold by a cord to the hearing aid. This type of aid is sometimes recommended for children with physical limitations when there is difficulty keeping the hearing aids on the ear and when there is great difficulty with feedback. However, there are some disadvantages of body aids to consider:

1. The microphone is not at ear level, and therefore does not provide natural sound reception at the ear.

2. Noise can result from clothes rubbing against the microphone,

3. If the body aid is worn on the chest, the microphone and controls can be damaged by food spills.

4. Parents also must be very careful, since the long cord can pose a strangulation risk if the cord is not secured in a manner to prevent this.

- What style is best for young children? Parents have noticed that many adults are now wearing very tiny hearing aids that fit inside the ear. Audiologists will almost always recommend a behind-the-ear hearing device for your child rather than an in-the-ear device. The casing for an in-the-ear device is made of a hard material — whereas the ear molds with behind-the-ear hearing aids are usually made out of soft material for children. (When a child falls or bumps his head, his ear is coming into contact with something soft, rather than something hard.) In addition, young children are continually growing. With an in-the-ear hearing aid you would have to pay for frequent changes to the casing as the size of your child's ear changed.

Hearing Aid Electronics (What's Inside The Hearing Aid)

- **Types of Hearing Aid Circuitry**
  The inside of the hearing aid has electronic parts to amplify and modify sound as it comes through the hearing aid. This "signal processor" is either analog or digital. An analog signal processor retains sound as waveforms; a digital signal processor converts sound into binary digits. Regardless of the signal processor used by the hearing aid, your audiologist determines the specifications your child requires in a hearing aid circuit.

  1. **Analog/Conventional** — The inside of the hearing aid has electronic parts to amplify and control sounds as they come through the hearing aid. Your audiologist determines the volume and other specifications your child requires in a hearing aid. This type of aid is not as flexible as either programmable or digital hearing aids. This is usually the least expensive type of hearing aid.

  2. **Analog/Programmable** — Your audiologist uses a computer to program your child's hearing aid. This makes these hearing aids more flexible. They can accommodate a wide range of hearing losses. If your child's hearing changes, the audiologist can often reprogram the hearing aid — which prevents having to buy a new hearing aid. These hearing aids typically offer more automatic adjustment for loud or soft sounds without having to use a volume control. Some programmable hearing aids are able to store different "programs" that are best for different listening situations (for instance, a quiet one-to-one situation — versus a noisy cafeteria). It would be difficult for a young child to independently make use of this feature.

3. **Digital/Programmable** — Digital hearing aids have a computer chip inside. This type of hearing aid is very flexible and allows the audiologist to "fine-tune" the hearing aid more precisely to fit your child's particular hearing loss. Digital hearing aids also allow for more adjustments to varying listening conditions. Manufacturers claim digital hearing aids have less distortion than analog hearing aids. This is usually the most expensive type of hearing aid.

WHICH TYPE OF HEARING AID IS BEST FOR MY CHILD?

Manufacturers of current digital aids offer aids that provide a more natural sound, reduced feedback problems, and present less difficulty in hearing in a noisy setting. Many adult hearing aid users report a much-improved sound with digital hearing aids. However, others prefer their analog hearing aids. Adult hearing aid users are able to report which hearing aid sounds best to them. Young children, however, cannot do this. Make sure your audiologist has expertise in fitting hearing aids on little ones. Your audiologist will help select the hearing aids he believes will be best for your child.

WHAT FEATURES ARE OFTEN RECOMMENDED FOR YOUNG CHILDREN?

Ask your audiologist if your child's hearing aids have these important features:

- Hearing aid is compatible for use with FM equipment and other Assistive Listening Devices.

- Hearing aid has tamper-resistant battery doors.

- Hearing aid has volume control cover.

SHOULD YOUR CHILD HAVE ONE OR TWO HEARING AIDS?

Most of the time two hearing aids are recommended for children who have a hearing loss in both ears. With two hearing aids a child may be better able to locate the source of sound and to hear better in a noisy setting. In addition, some research has indicated that when a child wears only one hearing aid, she may lose the ability to recognize speech in the other ear as the result of "auditory deprivation" in that ear.

BONE CONDUCTION HEARING AIDS

Most hearing aids are **air conduction** hearing aids which amplify sound into a child's ear canal. However, some children are unable to use **air conduction** hearing aids because their ear canals may be too narrow or may be closed off. These children use **bone conduction** hearing aids.

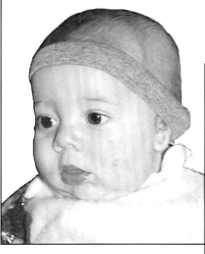
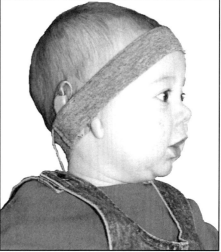

Child wearing a bone conduction hearing aid.

In **bone conduction** hearing aids, the electrical energy
of sound is changed into mechanical vibration, which
stimulates the bones of the child's skull. Through the bone
conduction hearing aid, sound is transmitted directly into
the **inner** part of a child's ear, bypassing the ear canal and
middle ear.

Here are some comments from the parents of a child who
used a bone conduction hearing aid —

> *"Getting the bone conduction hearing aid on Jesse early
> (he was two months old), really seems to have been the
> key in his acceptance of wearing it. We didn't see the
> benefits right away, but now (at six months) it's really
> paying off. We're seeing responses to sounds, and he
> wears it without fussing.*

> *"One of the problems we had to solve early on with the
> bone conduction aid was where and how to fasten the aid
> itself (the oscillator was held on by two-sided wig tape
> and the headband), because he was too young to wear the
> rigid metal headband. An additional challenge was that
> Jesse spit up a lot, and we didn't want the hearing aid to
> get wet. We ended up using a little clip-on bag which we
> could move from his chest to his shoulder, depending on
> his position (see photo). It worked fairly well, but there
> was much less hassle once he was sitting upright most of
> the time. Then we modified it to have both components
> (the aid itself and oscillator) in the headband.*

> *"We used a cotton Spandex headband to hold on the
> oscillator, which worked quite well; but the annoying part
> was that everybody thought he was a girl.*

> *"Jesse reached a stage when he was exploring his body.
> But fortunately he left his hearing aid alone, and he kept
> it on all the time he was awake. In fact, he seemed to need
> it to fall asleep, so we left it on and played music until he*

fell asleep and then we removed it. We think that Jesse's acceptance of his hearing aid was mainly due to the fact that he had worn it from such a young age (2 months) that it was like a part of his body.

"Although we appreciate it when people acknowledge that they've noticed the headband and/or hearing aid and have asked what it was for, it did get a little tiresome explaining over and over again and answering the same questions (for example, 'Can they correct it with surgery?'). Still, it was worth it if this means increasing people's awareness, and especially if it helps them to interact with Jesse more effectively."

BONE ANCHORED HEARING AID

A **bone anchored** hearing aid (**BAHA**) is for older children who have benefited from **bone conduction** hearing aids. A **BAHA** consists of a small titanium fixture that is inserted into the child's mastoid bone, just behind the ear. The fixture is made of a special material so that the bone bonds with it within a few months and it becomes securely attached. A small screw is connected to this fixture through the skin. The external part of the BAHA contains a tiny box with a microphone, processor and a battery — all attached to the screw. Sound vibrations are transmitted directly through the screw to the bone and from there to the cochlea.

What Are the Advantages of a BAHA Versus a Conventional Bone Conduction Hearing Aid?

Research shows that children receive an improved acoustical signal from the BAHA — compared to the conventional bone conduction hearing aid. In addition the BAHA is less visible, does not require the use of a headband, uses fewer batteries and is securely attached.

EARMOLDS

What Are Earmolds For?

The earmold, made from a soft material, fits snugly into the child's ear. It holds the hearing aid in place and directs the sound from the hearing aid into the child's ear canal.

How Long Do Earmolds Last?

As a baby grows, earmolds need to be replaced on a regular basis. Young children will often need frequent replacement of their earmolds. There is no hard-and-fast rule, but generally the younger the child and the more severe the hearing loss, the more frequently earmolds will need to be replaced. Many babies and young toddlers may need new earmolds every two or three months. Otoferm (a special type of silicone-based sealer) can sometimes be used temporarily to provide a little more seal until new molds can be made. Your Pediatric audiologist may have other solutions.

How Can You Tell When The Earmolds Need Replacing?

The high-pitched whistling sound coming from your child's hearing aid is called feedback. This happens when sound is escaping from the earmold and is picked up by the microphone and re-amplified. This feedback is often the signal that your child needs new earmolds or that the mold is improperly inserted. Accumulated earwax, which creates an obstruction and prevents sound from passing through the ear canal, can also cause feedback.

What Colour Should You Select?

Typically parents want to select a flesh-coloured earmold so that the hearing aids are less obvious. However, young children often delight in selecting their favourite from a variety of colours and will proudly "show off" their new colourful earmolds to others.

GETTING STARTED WITH HEARING AIDS

Once there is information about your child's hearing loss, an audiologist may recommend a hearing aid trial. For children who might benefit from cochlear implantation, the hearing aid trial may become part of the process to determine if your child will benefit more from a hearing aid or from a cochlear implant.

- Your audiologist will probably recommend that your child wear one or two hearing aids as much as possible every day.

- Beginning hearing aid use is sometimes difficult. Your child will need to learn to be aware of sound around him and to learn the meanings of those sounds. Every child reacts differently to wearing aids. Some accept them right away. Others would prefer to drop the aids in the nearest toilet bowl or garbage disposal.

From a parent:

"I found it important always to be the one to control when the hearing aids went in and out. So, if my child seemed to be getting tired of them, I'd take the aids out before he took them out. I would then put the aids on again after a half-hour break."

I can encourage my child to wear hearing aids during playtime.

- Using a water-based cream such as K-Y Jelly can make it easier to put the ear molds in. Do not use petroleum-based lubricants on silicone or other oil-based earmolds.

- Incorporate putting on your child's hearing aids into your morning routine. The earlier in the day this happens, the better. If you have an infant, you will likely be removing the hearing aids each time he takes a nap — then putting them back on during his waking hours. Older children also benefit from hearing aids being introduced first thing in the morning.

- Infants (less than six months) will often tolerate or accept full-time hearing aid use more quickly than older children.

- If your child pulls the aid off, stop whatever fun activity you're doing. Put the hearing aids back in. Continue the activity. Give your child lots of attention during the time he's wearing the hearing aids.

From a parent:

"I began introducing the aids slowly in quieter situations at first. I would carefully select which sounds he would be exposed to."

From a parent:

"We bought a new toy car for our daughter to sit in while we put the hearing aids on. This helped to distract her."

From a parent:

"During the first week, we put the hearing aids on while our son sat in his high-chair eating little marshmallows."

A fun activity can distract my child when I put the hearing aids on.

- Gradually increase the amount of time your child wears his hearing aids. Leave the hearing aids on as long as he is comfortable.

- Help your child get used to the sounds around him as quickly as possible. But use your own judgment to determine how fast to go with your child. Babies are less aware of their bodies and adapt more readily to the use of a hearing aid. Some toddlers and preschool children may take more time to become used to wearing hearings aids. It may be better to take three or four weeks to let your child get used to wearing hearing aids all day — instead of spending one week pushing your child into full-time use, only to find you must continue fighting with him for the next two years. Some children can develop a negative attitude if they associate hearing aids with battles.

It is best for your young child to learn that you are in charge of taking hearing aids out. If possible, try to be the one to remove the hearing aids — rather than your child. Observe your child. Just before he seems ready to take his hearing aids off, praise him for wearing the aids, and then take them off. Removing the hearing aids before your child does, helps to reinforce hearing aid **use** instead of hearing aid **removal**.

- If getting the hearing aids on is a struggle, try to keep the following hints in mind:

  1. Select a moment when you both are well rested.

  2. Spend time with your child in an activity he enjoys.

  3. Put the hearing aids on for short periods at first.

  4. Praise your child for keeping the aids in. If your child pulls the aids out, stop the fun activity

and calmly put the hearing aids back in. If your child again refuses to allow you to put the aids in, stop the fun activity and let your child know you will try once more later that day.

- **Goal:** Hearing aids go on your child first thing in the morning and are taken off only for bathtime or bed. Sometimes it helps to break this goal up into smaller, more workable steps. The time it takes to reach the goal of full-time hearing aid use is different for each child and family.

KEEPING HEARING AIDS ON

Parents of babies and active toddlers may find it a real challenge to keep hearing aids on their child. Here are some devices that many parents have found helpful. The first four items help to keep the hearing aids properly in place on your child's head. The last four devices help to prevent the loss of hearing aids.

Baby/Toddler Bonnet

A bonnet helps prevent your baby from pulling the hearing aid off her ears — yet does not distort sounds coming into the hearing aid. But a hood on a coat does seem to distort sound by producing noise as the cloth rubs against the microphone. Also, a hood can sometimes cause the aid to squeal.

To make a bonnet, see patterns and instructions on the following pages.

Basic Bonnet Construction

Items needed other than fabric:

- About 8 inches (20 cm) of iron-on interfacing

From a parent:

"During the first year, every time we'd get new earmolds, our child would again rebel against the hearing aids."

From a parent;

"During that first year we were most concerned about our child's health. He was in and out of the hospital so many times. We didn't have the energy to think about hearing aids until a few months later."

From a parent:

"Sometimes I felt like such a failure. I knew hearing aids were important, but I just couldn't keep them on her. I felt better when I talked with two other parents of kids who, like my daughter, have Down Syndrome. Those families also had a hard time keeping aids on at first."

- 4 inches of 3/8 inch-wide elastic thread

- 16 inches of bias tape (1/4 inch wide)

Procedure:

- First cut a piece of 3/8 inch-wide elastic 4 inches long.

- Iron bonnet top at appropriate folding lines (shown on pattern piece), and sew on stitching lines as indicated. Weave elastic through casing with safety pin, and sew across each end to hold elastic in place.

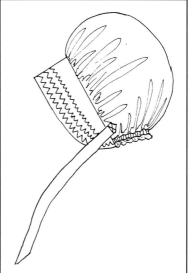

- Sew in dart on bonnet top. Iron.

- Iron interfacing onto bonnet cap, and sew cap along curved side (apply decorative stitching if you wish).

- Sew two rows of gathering stitches (as indicated on bonnet-top pattern piece) from circle to circle.

- Tighten gathers enough to match notches on bonnet cap. Sew cap on completely. Trim and finish seam allowance with bias tape.

- Hem bonnet straps by turning under hem allowance twice.

- Sew straps onto top of bonnet at indicated positions.

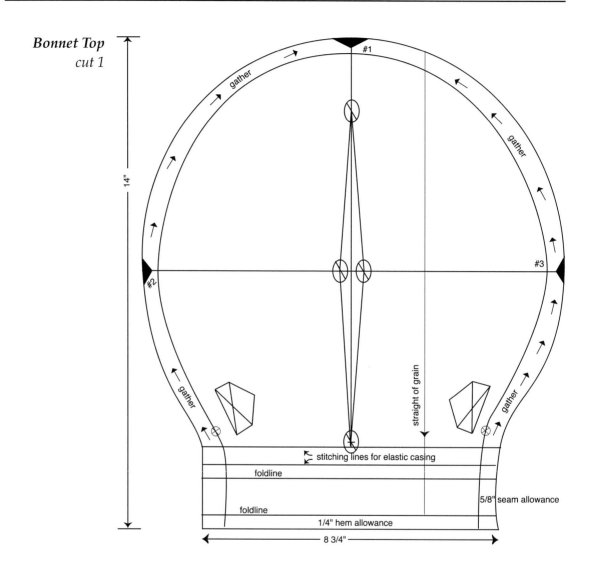

Bonnet Top
cut 1

14"

gather

gather

#1

#2

#3

gather

gather

straight of grain

stitching lines for elastic casing

foldline

foldline

5/8" seam allowance

1/4" hem allowance

8 3/4"

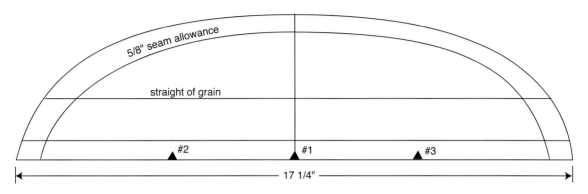

Bonnet Cap
cut 2 of fabric
cut 2 of interfacing

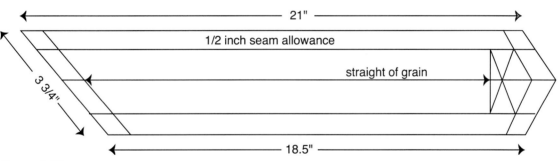

Bonnet Strap
cut 2

Headband

Some parents use headbands to help keep their child's hearing aids in place. Make sure the headband does not cover up the microphone of the hearing aid (ask your audiologist to point it out).

Huggie Aids

These are rings of plastic tubing designed to keep the aids on small children and to protect the controls and battery compartment.

Some parents report liking the Huggie Aid, while others say that their children hate it. Some feel more secure knowing that their child would have greater difficulty getting into the battery compartment. A few parents complain that the Huggie Aids make their child's ears stick out. One problem seems to be that Huggie Aids are sometimes fitted improperly (often too small). This makes the Huggie part more uncomfortable than the hearing aids.

Source: Audiology clinic or hearing aid dealer.

Wig/Toupee Tape

Two-sided, skin-sensitive tape helps keep the hearing aids in place behind the ears of an active child. It helps prevent the aids from "flopping" around.

Source: Wig shop, hairdresser — possibly a large pharmacy.

Fishing Line

Loop one end of fishing line around the hook of the hearing aid. Tie the other end to a safety pin and attach it to the middle of the back of your child's shirt. If he pulls the hearing aids out, they'll dangle from his back — instead of getting lost in the grass!

Source: Tackle shop or Dad's fishing box.

From a parent:

"Fishing line did not work with our toddler. He would just hook his little fingers around the hoop of line and use it as a handle to pull the aid off."

From a Parent:

"We used an eye-glass sports strap that wrapped around the back of her head to keep the hearing aids on. We then connected the strap to the back of her shirt with safety pins and fishing line."

Eyeglass Strap

To use an eyeglass strap, take tubing apart at the ear molds. Slip on the ends of the eyeglass strap — then reattach tubing. Pin strap to back of shirt. Ask your audiologist or hearing-aid technician about attaching a cord directly to the earmold during the making of the mold.

Source: Optician or drug store.

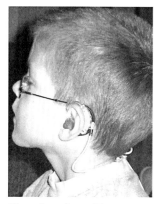

Keep hearing aids on with eyeglasses strap.

Stampede String

This string (like an eyeglass strap, but used by cowboys to keep their hats on) has alligator clips on the end that can clip onto the plastic ring of a Huggie Aid. The other end is attached to a safety pin, which is then clipped to the back of the child's shirt — about midway between the shoulder blades.

Fun OtoClips®

These lightweight cords attach easily to the hearing instrument — then clip securely to the child's clothing. The clips are covered with pictures of familiar animals, sea creatures, and dinosaurs. (Phone: 719/540-9333 or www.westone.com/kids.html).

Ear Gear

There are "Ear Gear" sleeves for hearing aid casings available that cover the body of the hearing aid and then attach with a cord and clip to the child's clothing. (Toll free in the U.S. and Canada: 1-888-766-1838)

Stick-On, Child "Earrings"

Many toy stores sell tiny, colourful stickers that little girls use for pretend earrings. Parents of deaf or hard of hearing toddlers like to stick these appealing stickers onto the hearing aids. You can place a different colour onto each aid so that you can easily recognize which aid is for the left ear and which is for the right. Parents also report that it makes their job much easier when they're searching for a lost aid in a beige carpet. Brightly coloured earmolds also make it much easier to find lost earmolds or lost hearing aids.

If you have tried some of the devices mentioned in this chapter and your child's hearing aids are still flopping off his ear, ask your audiologist to check the length of your child's tubing. You might also want to ask your audiologist for the names of parents who've gone through this same experience. Some children with specific syndromes may have flaccid ears and can have particular difficulty keeping hearing aids on. Ask your audiologist to help you solve this problem.

If you live in BC, we can help to connect you with other families through a **Parent-to-Parent Support Network.** You can write or call:

Toll Free: 1-877-584-2827 (voice)
604-584-2827 (voice)
604-584-9108 (tty)

Write: BC Family Hearing Resource Centre
Parent-to-Parent Support Network
15220 – 92nd Avenue
Surrey, BC V3R 2T8
Web: www.bcfamilyhearing.com

If you live in the United States you can contact the **Hands and Voices** organization to talk with other parents.

Web: www.handsandvoices.org
Phone: 866-422-0422 (Toll free)

From a parent:

"We put colourful earring stickers on our son's hearing aids. But we use only the happy face 'earring' stickers, rather than the ones with pink flowers on them."

CHAPTER 6

LEARNING MORE ABOUT HEARING AIDS

What If My Child Continues to Reject His Hearing Aids? 73
Observing My Child's Responses to Sound 76
Checking and Cleaning to Make Sure the Hearing Aids Work 79
Help! My Child's Hearing Aids Is Not Working 84
What Equipment Do I Need? 86
Emergency: My Child Swallowed a Battery 87
FM Systems 88

WHAT IF MY CHILD CONTINUES TO REJECT HEARING AIDS?

Wearing aids is a new experience for your child. He may not yet be used to the feel of the earmold or to the new sounds he is listening to. Whenever possible, involve your child in the process by explaining what is happening. If he is old enough, let him make choices such as the colour of the earmolds. Earmolds are now available in colours like pink and green that are fun for children.

Use the following checklist to help you determine why your child might be rejecting the hearing aids.

WHY MY CHILD MIGHT BE REJECTING HIS HEARING AIDS

FIND OUT   YES/NO?

Are the aids working properly?   _____

Hint: If not, have the aids repaired.

Is the volume of the aid set correctly?   _____

Hint: If not, adjust volume to level set by audiologist or ask audiologist to re-evaluate level.

Are the batteries good?   _____

Hint: Check batteries every day with battery tester.

Do the earmolds fit comfortably?   _____

Hint: If the tubing sticks out beyond the opening of the earmold, ask the audiologist or technician to sand it down.

Hint: If the molds keep falling out, inquire about "softer" earmold material and about using Otoferm, a silicone sealant.

Hint: If there is any acoustic feedback (squealing), check that the earmolds fit snugly. They may need to be re-inserted or your growing child may need new earmolds.

Hint: Ask your audiologist or pediatrician to check for wax build up in the ear canal (do not attempt to remove it yourself).

Are the aids adjusted properly so that they are not causing sounds to be too loud or not loud enough?   _____

Hint: Check with your audiologist.

Do the hearing aids keep falling off?   _____

Hint: Try some of the devices mentioned earlier.

Does my child have sensitive skin or skin allergies?   _____

Hint: If your child's ears look sore or red, ask your audiologist about hypo-allergenic earmolds. The audiologist should also look at the mold for some "high" spots that may be rubbing on the skin. It might be possible to sand this high spot down.

WHY MY CHILD MIGHT BE REJECTING HIS HEARING AIDS (CONT'D)

FIND OUT   YES/NO?

Is my child sick with an ear infection or other illness?   _____

Hint: This is not a good time to push hearing aid use.

Is my child too tired, excited, or worried when I put the aids in?   _____

Hint: Wait until you both feel calm, rested, and are not in a hurry.

Do I feel comfortable and confident?   _____

*Hint: Often children can sense it when we are uncomfortable or have
negative feelings. Your own attitude about the hearing aids may influence
your child's willingness to wear them.*

Do I have mixed emotions about these hearing aids?   _____

*Hint: If you feel your child really doesn't need the hearing aids, ask your
audiologist to evaluate your child again. Ask the audiologist to show you
what levels of speech your child is able to hear - with and without hearing
aids.*

Am I in a power struggle with my child?   _____

*Hint: Initial hearing aid use is often a stressful time for many parents
Frequently, young children learn they can get the upper hand by pulling
out the hearing aids and refusing to wear them.*

*Hint: Talk to other parents, and find out how they handled this difficult
time. Often, you can learn successful ideas from other parents — which
professionals have never thought of. Use our toll-free number to phone
or write to the BC Family Hearing Resource Centre Parent-to-Parent
Support Network to make contact with other families of deaf and hard of
hearing children.*

**Is my child going through a hearing aid trial prior to being
considered for cochlear implant?**   _____

*Hint: Your child's rejection of the hearing aids could mean he is not
benefiting enough from the hearing aids.*

OBSERVING MY CHILD'S RESPONSES TO SOUND

Listed on the following chart are ways that children show they are aware of sound when they are wearing hearing aids. When and how your child responds to sound may depend on the severity of his hearing loss, as well as the length of time he has been wearing hearing aids.

Your child has a better chance of becoming aware of sounds if —

- You eliminate background noise (for example, dishwasher, TV, washing machine).

- You bring your child closer to the sound. (Stay near your child when you talk with him.)

- You make your child more aware of sound. (See Chapter 8, "Bringing My Child's Attention to Sound and Making Sound Meaningful.")

Typical Responses That Show My Child Is Aware of Sound

Listed in the following chart are ways that children typically show an awareness of sound — including voices — after hearing aids are put on. You may not observe these responses for many weeks — or even months — after your child begins wearing hearing aids full time. A very small number of children may have such a profound hearing loss that they will never demonstrate these responses even when using hearing aids.

In order to record your child's progress for your audiologist, enter the date on which you make the following observations.

CHILD'S REACTION

DATE *When wearing hearing aids, my child —*

_____ Becomes **quieter** during the first few weeks.

_____ **Cries** immediately following sound or voice.

_____ **Reacts** in some subtle way to sound. For example, his eyes blink or he briefly stops activity.

_____ **Enjoys** toys and activities that make noise (drum, taped music).

_____ **Searches** around or **looks up** from play after a sound has occurred.

_____ **Uses voice** (coos, gurgles) more when wearing hearing aids.

_____ **Indicates** when he hears something — for example, points to his ear.

_____ **Reacts** in some way when a sound **stops**.

_____ **Turns** when his name is called.

_____ **Imitates** my voice or speech.

HEARING AID USE: MY PERSONAL CHART

Parents should keep track of their child's response to sound while he is wearing his hearing aids so progress can be evaluated.

DAY	ACTIVITY	OBSERVATIONS/CONCERNS/ QUESTIONS
SUNDAY		
MONDAY		
TUESDAY		
WEDNESDAY		
THURSDAY		
FRIDAY		
SATURDAY		

CHECKING AND CLEANING TO MAKE SURE THE HEARING AIDS WORK

Why Check and Clean?

- Checking and maintaining hearing aids on a regular basis may prevent time-consuming trips to the audiologist or hearing aid dealer for repair services.

- Checking the aids ensures aids are providing optimal benefit to your child.

- Putting a hearing aid on your child that is not working properly is worse than his having no hearing aid at all.

- A crackling, scratching, or intermittent sound signal will confuse or frustrate your child and can cause him to reject the aid.

When Should I Do It?

- Check your batteries every day. Using a battery tester is the most reliable way to test batteries.

- As your child gets older, consider involving him in the process of daily listening checks. At first, he can just observe. Slowly, include your child by asking him to help you with battery checks, washing earmolds, and saying speech sounds as you listen through the stethoscope. Your goal is to assist your child in becoming an independent and responsible hearing aid user. Some children as young as three can put in their earmolds and check the batteries.

How Can I Make Sure the Hearing Aid is Working?

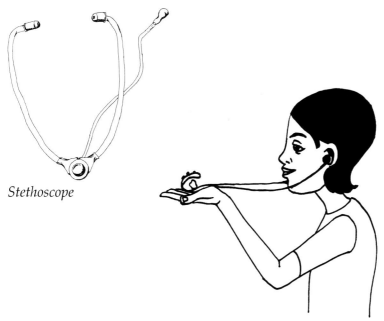

Stethoscope

I can use a stethoscope for a daily listening check of my child's hearing aids.

How Do I Do a Listening Check?

By becoming familiar with how the aids should sound, you will later be able to notice any differences — distorted sound, lowered volume — that would mean the hearing aids are in need of repair.

- Turn the hearing aid to "O" (off), and turn the volume control down (so you won't blast your own ears with a loud sound).

- Attach the hearing aid to the stethoscope. You can do this with or without the earmold still connected. If you remove the earmold, just connect the hook to the end of the stethoscope to listen. (See sketch.)

- Turn the hearing aid to "M" (microphone) and slowly turn volume up to a comfortable level.

- Hold the aid about six inches from your mouth and say a few words into the microphone. Listen to the sound.

- Say the six following sounds, known as the "Ling 6 Sounds," into the microphone. This six-sound test allows you to hear the hearing aid's output across the speech range.

  OOO — AH — EEE — SH — SSS — MMMM

  1. OOO (as in *who*)

  2. AH (as in *art*)

  3. EEE (as in *eat*)

  4. SH (as in *she*)

  5. SSS (as in *so*)

  6. MMMM (as in *moo*).

MAKING SURE THE HEARING AID IS WORKING

LISTENING CHECK

_____ Is the sound clear and without distortion?

_____ Are there any sudden jumps in loudness when you turn the volume control?

_____ Is the sound scratchy?

_____ Does the sound cut in and out?

For trouble-shooting hints, see the section in this chapter, *Help! My Child's Hearing Aid is Not Working.*

VISUAL CHECK

Battery

_____ Does battery tester say battery is still good?

_____ Are battery contacts clean?

_____ Can you match the + on battery to the + on battery compartment?

Case

_____ No chips, cracks, flaws?

_____ Does it shut completely?

Tubing

_____ No cracks, holes, stiffness?

_____ Not twisted?

_____ Free of moisture?

Hook

_____ Does it fit tightly into mold and aid?

Earmold

_____ Clean?

_____ Hole drilled in mold canal free of wax and moisture?

Keep this in mind: Just a couple of drops of moisture in the tubing or earmold can greatly reduce the loudness of the sound your child receives.

How Do I Stop Feedback (Whistling)

- If there is an "air leak" around the earmold edge (usually because the earmold is too small or is improperly inserted), use a special cream product such as Otoferm. Put a tiny bit of the cream around the outer edge of the earmold before inserting the hearing aid on your child to help maintain a seal.

- If the earmold appears to be too small, make an appointment with your audiologist, hearing aid dealer, or technician to get your child fitted with new molds. Check for accumulated wax or debris that might be causing the blockage.

- It's not unusual for young children to require new molds frequently (every three to six months).

How Do I Clean My Child's Earmold?

- Check for wax every day. Wax in or on a mold can make the hearing aid whistle or become ineffective.

- Do not use toothpicks, pins, or pipe cleaners, as they can scratch or tear earmolds.

- Daily, wipe earmold with a slightly damp cloth.

- Weekly, wash earmold in warm, soapy water. Use a wet toothbrush for washing away heavy wax.

How Do I Clean My Child's Hearing Aid?

- Wipe case clean with a soft cloth.

- Use a dry toothbrush to brush away dirt and food from the microphone.

- Clean the contacts of the hearing aid with a pencil eraser or with a contact cleaning solution. Ask your audiologist or hearing aid dealer about cleaning solutions appropriate for cleaning the contacts. (Note: do not use contact lens cleaning solution!)

- Allow earmold to dry completely before reattaching to the hearing aid. A small squeeze-ball blower can assist with clearing any water trapped inside.

HELP! MY CHILD'S HEARING AID IS NOT WORKING

If you're unable to successfully trouble-shoot your child's hearing aid, call your audiologist or hearing aid dealer immediately. Describe the problem and ask for advice. If you are still unable to solve the problem, take the aid in for repair and ask to borrow a loaner aid that is equivalent to your child's own aid.

Sometimes electrical problems are intermittent (they come and go). This can be very frustrating if you are unable to demonstrate the problem to the audiologist or hearing aid dealer. It may help if you have a record of all problems.

Write down the date and the problems you are experiencing. Make a copy to give to the audiologist or hearing aid dealer.

The following chart can help you trouble-shoot your child's hearing aid and find possible solutions to problems.

Troubleshooting Hearing Aids

WHAT IF ...?	TO CHECK OR DO
The volume does not get louder.	Is battery still good? **Test it.**
Sound goes on and off intermittently or there is a sudden jump in loudness when you turn the volume control.	Phone audiologist/hearing aid dealer.
Sound is muffled.	Twisted tube? **Untwist it.** Wax in earmold? **Clean mold.** Did the aid get wet? **Blow it out.** Is there moisture in the tube? **Dry it.**
Sound is scratchy.	Phone audiologist/hearing aid dealer.
Sound is rattling.	Check tube: Is it bent or twisted? Any holes? **Replace broken tubing.**
No sound.	Is switch on "M"? Is battery good and inserted correctly? Has aid been immersed in water, or is it extremely damp from moisture? **If so, call audiologist or hearing aid dealer.**
You hear feedback (whistling, high-pitched sound) when your child has the aid on.	Is earmold inserted properly in your child's ear? **Push in again.** Is there a hole in tubing or a crack in the hearing aid case? **Replace the tubing.** Has your child outgrown this earmold? **Get new mold.** Did you turn volume up past the prescribed setting? **Turn volume to correct setting.**

WHAT EQUIPMENT DO I NEED?

Here is a list of equipment that you may find helpful for checking the aids or doing simple cleaning. You may not need all of these items. Talk with your audiologist if you have any questions.

Some parents find it easier to keep these supplies together in one place, such as a plastic storage box.

ITEM AND PURPOSE	SOURCE
Stethoscope: Lets you listen through the hearing aid. Looks similar to the stethoscope used by doctors to listen to your heartbeat.	Audiologist or hearing aid dealer.
Battery Tester: Lets you check to see if batteries are good or need replacing. Using a battery tester is more reliable than just listening for acoustic feedback from the hearing aid. Sometimes batteries that are "almost" dead will still allow a hearing aid to squeal when you turn it on. Don't test for more than about two seconds because the tester can draw power from the battery.	Audiologist, hearing aid dealer, or electronic equipment store.
Spare Batteries: So you can replace dead or weak batteries immediately. Purchase type recommended by audiologist.	Audiologist, hearing aid dealer, or drug store.
Pencil-type Typewriter Eraser: To clean battery contacts.	Office supply store or drug store.
Blower for Earmolds: To blow out moisture from mold and tubing after washing (also used for cleaning cameras).	Audiologist, hearing aid dealer, or camera shop.
Hearing Aid Drying Kit: To store aid in overnight. Removes moisture from aids and molds and extends life of aids.	Audiologist or hearing aid dealer.
Small Soft Toothbrush: Allows you to clean molds thoroughly.	Drug store.

Battery Management

Batteries are the lifeblood of your hearing aids. Here are some suggestions for their maintenance.

- Store batteries in a cool dry place. Don't store them in the refrigerator, because the refrigerator is damp and the moisture can deteriorate the seal on the battery tab.

- Avoid handling batteries for extended periods of time before inserting them into the hearing aid. The oils on your skin may get into the holes on the top of the battery and clog them.

- Avoid carrying loose batteries in your pocket with coins and keys. Contact with metal items can short out the battery.

- Safely dispose of corroded batteries.

- Put batteries in your child's hearing aids correctly (the "+" on the battery should match the "+" on the battery door).

- Avoid buying more than a three-months supply at one time.

- Safely dispose of dead batteries.

EMERGENCY: MY CHILD SWALLOWED A BATTERY!

Yes, Batteries Are Poisonous.

If your child swallows a battery, take him to a hospital or medical emergency room promptly.

What Should You Take With You To The Emergency Room?

Bring along the empty battery container — or a new battery, the same as the one he swallowed.

What Might Happen At The Emergency Room?

An x-ray may be taken to determine the location of the battery.

Most frequently the battery will be "on its way through" (in the stomach), and the parents will be told to check their child's bowel movements in order to locate the battery. If, however, the battery is lodged somewhere (for instance, in the esophagus), a minor surgical procedure may be performed without delay.

Important! If your child later shows symptoms of stomach discomfort or pain, take him back to the hospital **immediately.**

FM SYSTEMS

What is an FM System?

An FM works in the same way we use a radio: a transmitter and microphone worn by the speaker acts as the radio station, and a receiver worn by the child using hearing aids acts as the radio. The child's receiver picks up the signal from the talker's microphone and transmits it to the child's hearing aid or cochlear implant processor. With many FM systems coupled to hearing aids, there are three options for settings.

- When the FM is turned off, the child hears only through his hearing aid.

- When the FM is turned on and the hearing aids are turned on, the child hears the talker using a microphone at a louder level than other noises. This option of FM plus hearing aid allows the child to benefit from hearing several different talkers, such as at circle time when the preschool teacher is wearing a microphone and other children are taking turns talking during share and tell.

- The third option is FM only. Only the sounds through the FM transmitting microphone are amplified. All background noise is thereby eliminated. In the preschool situation, the child would hear only the teacher and would not hear any other sound in the classroom, including comments from other children.

Types of FM systems

- Personal FM

  There are a variety of personal FM systems available. Some FM receivers are worn on the body and look like a Walkman. Other, very small FM systems, are connected directly to the child's ear-level hearing aid. Your pediatric audiologist can determine if your child would benefit from an FM system and can advise you of the type of system that would be most appropriate for your child.

  If your child uses a Walkman type of FM you may want to use a pouch similar to the one shown here.

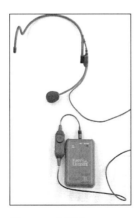

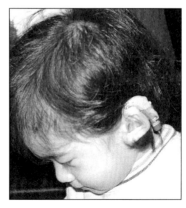

Personal FM transmitter

Personal FM in body worn pouch

Cordless personal FM receiver

- Sound-Field System

  A classroom sound-field system is essentially a public address (PA) system with the inclusion of a wireless (FM) microphone for the teacher.

  As the teacher talks into the microphone, her voice is broadcast through loudspeakers — usually placed on the walls of the classroom — allowing her to move around the room and still be heard at constant levels throughout the classroom. With this system, all the children — regardless of seat location and the direction the teacher is facing — are able to hear the teacher above the background sounds.

  There are also small, portable sound-field systems that can be placed on the desk of a student. These sound-field systems are typically used for children who are unable to use a personal FM system.

  Children with moderate or greater hearing loss would benefit more from a personal FM system than from a classroom sound-field system, although some children with cochlear implants and some children with temporary conductive hearing losses do benefit from the use of sound-field systems.

What are the benefits of FM?

In ideal listening conditions, such as the audiologist's sound-proof booth, your child may hear well with her hearing aids alone. However, background noise, distance between the listener and speaker, and echoes or reverberation off walls and floors occur in every-day listening experience — diminishing understanding. Even hearing children have trouble paying attention in a noisy room. Those with hearing loss have even more difficulty.

Although it is important for your child to experience a variety of listening conditions, there is also an overwhelming amount of evidence on the negative impact that distance and noise has on communication development. Frequency Modulated (FM) systems allow your child to hear without the distraction of noise — as if the talker were speaking about six inches from the child's hearing aid, even though the talker is much further away.

In recent years sound absorbing carpets in public schools have been removed to accommodate children with allergies, and new schools have been built with such features as vaulted ceilings and skylights in hallways. Actions such as these have contributed to poor acoustics in schools. Children with a hearing loss have particular difficulty in rooms with poor acoustics. Typical preschools and kindergartens are very noisy environments. Several children are often talking at the same time and frequently moving from one activity to another.

Hearing children acquire many language skills from overhearing conversations and speech while they move around from place to place. For this reason, an FM system can help to make this incidental learning possible for a young child with hearing loss — when the distance between him and others changes constantly.

FM systems used in a daycare situation (for example, when the caregiver is telling a story) can be helpful in keeping a young child's attention. In addition, by using FM systems during the preschool years a young child becomes more familiar with the equipment and may adjust more quickly to the equipment in kindergarten.

Uses of an FM System

Your pediatric audiologist can determine the advantage for your child using an FM system and can also give you

information about the variety of personal FM systems that
are available.

CHAPTER 7

COCHLEAR IMPLANTS

What Is a Cochlear Implant? 93
How Does a Cochlear Implant Work? 94
Would My Child Benefit From a Cochlear Implant? 96
Preparing for the Cochlear Implant 97
After Your Child's Surgery 99
Controlling Electrostatic Discharge (ESD) 100
More Cochlear Implant Precautions 101
*Checklist for Proper Care of the Cochlear
    Implant Device* 102
*Helping My Child to Identify and Prevent Problems With the
    System* 105
Observing My Child's Behaviour 106
*Assessing the Environment To Make Learning
    Optimal* 107
Assistive Listening Devices and Cochlear Implants 107

WHAT IS A COCHLEAR IMPLANT?

A cochlear implant is an electronic implantable device consisting of internal and external parts. Its purpose is to provide sound detection and speech recognition when it has been determined that there is little or no benefit from hearing aids for your child.

The external parts include a **microphone** to pick up sound, a **speech processor** to analyze the sounds, and a **headpiece** to transmit the sound to the implant.

The internal, implanted parts include the **receiver** and the **electrode array.**

The internal parts are surgically implanted under the skin during a two-to-three-hour operation under general anesthesia. The electrode array is surgically inserted into the cochlea (the bony casing that forms the inner ear). The receiver is embedded under the skin behind the designated ear and connected to the electrode array in the cochlea.

The headpiece magnetically attaches to the surface of the head behind the ear where the internal receiver is located under the skin. The ear-level microphone and ear-level or body-worn speech processor are connected to the headpiece by an electrical cord.

Between four to six weeks after the surgery, when the incision has healed, the device is activated with internal and external parts working together for the first time. When the whole system is in place and turned on, it provides sound information to the child's brain by directly stimulating the auditory nerve fibers where damaged or absent hair cells normally would provide that function.

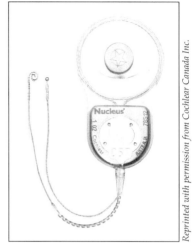

Cochlear Implant internal parts

HOW DOES A COCHLEAR IMPLANT WORK?

The internal and externals parts change sound into electrical signals that are carried to the brain by the hearing nerve where they are interpreted as sound. It happens so quickly that the listener does not experience any delay in hearing speech and other sounds. The way the cochlear implant works can be described as six steps:

1. The microphone picks up sounds and transmits the sound energy through the cord to the speech processor.

2. The speech processor analyzes and digitizes the sound energy into a code that is sent back through the cord to the headpiece. The digital code is transmitted across the skin, via radio waves, to the internal receiver underneath the skin.

3. The internal receiver sends the radio frequency information to the electrodes that have been inserted inside the cochlea.

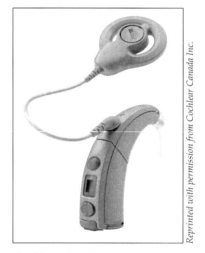

Cochlear Implant external parts

4. The electrodes send electrically charged signals directly to the auditory nerve, bypassing damaged parts of the cochlea.

5. The auditory nerve carries the signals to the auditory area of the brain.

6. The brain interprets the signals as sound.

The surgery and first activation is just the beginning of a long process of hearing habilitation and education for the child and family. The cochlear implant is recognized as an effective intervention for children with profound or severe-to-profound hearing loss when amplification with hearing aids is not adequate.

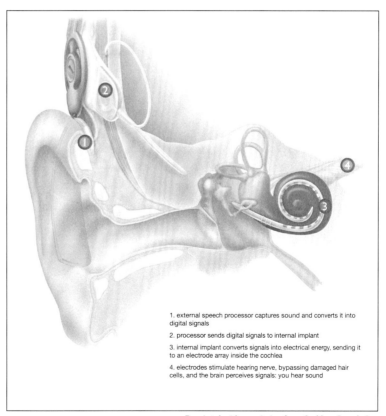

1. external speech processor captures sound and converts it into digital signals

2. processor sends digital signals to internal implant

3. internal implant converts signals into electrical energy, sending it to an electrode array inside the cochlea

4. electrodes stimulate hearing nerve, bypassing damaged hair cells, and the brain perceives signals: you hear sound

How a Cochlear Implant Works

Reprinted with permission from Cochlear Canada Inc.

WOULD MY CHILD BENEFIT FROM A COCHLEAR IMPLANT?

Members of your child's cochlear implant team, in collaboration with you and your child's community-based team of professionals, will determine whether your child is a cochlear implant candidate. Parents tell us that when they are gathering information and trying to make decisions they believe it is very important to:

- Have a member on the team who knows their child and family. This may be a speech-language pathologist, auditory-verbal therapist, or another professional.

- Have contact with a surgeon experienced with implant operations.

- Contact community therapists or teachers who have been, or are willing to be, trained to (re)habilitate cochlear implant recipients, and who are able to communicate well with their child.

Common concerns of parents:

- Risks of surgery

  "I felt somewhat relieved when we learned the rate of surgical complications associated with the cochlear implant procedure is extremely low. The major risk is associated with the general anesthetic."

- Success rate

  "We were worried that our son might not be any better off with the cochlear implant, but decided that we needed to try. Then, at least, we would never wonder if he could have benefited from the implant."

- Time commitment and financial strain

"I decided to ask for a change in my work schedule so that I would be able to participate in Leah's auditory-verbal therapy sessions and attend a support group for parents, but I was worried I would get burned-out."

PREPARING FOR THE COCHLEAR IMPLANT

Parents often report feeling anxious and worried in the time before their child receives the implant. This is a natural reaction. But it helps to calm "jitters" if you spend the time leading up to the surgery in getting prepared. Here are some of the things you can do:

- See that your child wears his hearing aids during all of his waking hours in the weeks before the surgery. This will help auditory nerve stimulation and will accustom your child to wearing his cochlear implant.

- Carefully consider your own feelings about a cochlear implant for your child — your expectations, hopes and concerns. Following the implant surgery, your child will need to wear his new device all the time, except when he sleeps. At first, he will not recognize a sound or word. So you can expect a period of adjustment as he adapts to the new hearing sensations — entirely different from what he experienced with his hearing aid. During this time, he will need instruction in auditory training techniques to develop new listening skills.

- Consider, also, the factors that play a role in how much your child may benefit from a cochlear implant.

    – Your child's age at the onset of deafness.

    – The formation of structures of the cochlea itself and the extent of nerve-fiber damage.

    – The period of time your child has been deaf with minimal benefit from hearing aids and a lack of progress in auditory development.

    – Your child's learning style.

    – Your child's age at implantation.

    – Realistic expectations for the child's development and performance with the cochlear implant.

    – Knowledge of how the implant works.

    – Emotional adjustment to your child's hearing loss and need for a cochlear implant.

    – Commitment to habilitative therapy, as well as ongoing audiological programming (which involves fine-tuning the device).

    – Support and encouragement from the family and community for your child to use his new device to stimulate his auditory development.

- Contact other cochlear implant users (and non-users), especially deaf and hard of hearing adults. Seek their views about cochlear implant use.

- Network with other parents whose children use cochlear implants. Become involved with associations related to hearing loss and the use of implants (see Appendix).

- Discuss appropriate vaccinations for meningitis with your surgeon and cochlear implant team.

From parents of children with cochlear implants:

"I was hoping the hearing aids would give Jaime enough benefit, because the thought of going through surgery for a cochlear implant when he was so little really scared me. It helped to meet another infant who had been implanted, and to hear her Dad say that she recovered so quickly after the surgery and went home the next day."

"It was such a relief to get past the surgical procedure. Looking back, that was the easiest part. My son's scar took longer to heal than usual, but other than that, the surgery was over and done with so quickly relative to the years of rehabilitation."

"There was never any question in my mind about getting the cochlear implant. If our daughter needed to learn to listen with a surgically implanted device, then that was what we would do. I was not without my fears, but I had more hope than anything. I think that's what kept me going."

From parents of children with cochlear implants:

"I have no regrets about getting a cochlear implant for Travis. All the energy spent in listening and speech therapy paid off, and we wouldn't be where we are today without the implant."

"I know that Lyla would not be talking without the cochlear implant. Even so, we have a long way to go, and I am still worried about how easily and clearly she will be able to communicate with others when she goes to kindergarten next year."

- Plan how you will manage the potential for electrostatic discharge (ESD) damage to the cochlear implant device (see ESD in the Glossary of terms). Learn about the sources of static electricity and how to prevent static electricity buildup to harmful levels. Many families of young children avoid plastic play equipment altogether.

AFTER YOUR CHILD'S SURGERY

Some of the challenges you will face when your child first wears his cochlear implant may seem overwhelming. But, as other parents report, in time everything becomes far easier.

About a month after surgery, your audiologist will create a listening program called a "MAP" to store in the speech processor. This is the first of a series of sessions to program the map to match your child's unique needs. Depending on the age of your child, don't expect to leave the first mapping session with a complete map that won't need changes. It is common to have eight to twelve mapping sessions over the first few years of implant use, and up to 20 visits with the audiologist during the first three years of implant use.

As mentioned earlier, don't expect your child to recognize or respond favourably to sound at first. The hearing sensation is a totally new experience for your child and is often frightening. Many young children are upset and attempt to remove the device, because they fear this strange, new sensation is out of their control.

Ask your audiologist if your child should continue to use a hearing aid on the non-implanted ear for ongoing stimulation. You may also want to ask about bilateral cochlear implants (an implant for each ear). If your audiologist recommends *against* using a hearing aid on the non-implanted ear, you may find your child reluctant to give up the hearing aid until he has adjusted to the new hearing sensation provided by the cochlear implant.

CONTROLLING ELECTROSTATIC DISCHARGE (ESD)

What Is Electrostatic Discharge (ESD), and What Can We Do About It?

Static electricity can damage the electrical parts of the cochlear implant system or corrupt programs (MAPs) in the speech processor.

Precautions to avoid discharge of static electricity to the cochlear implant device include:

- Always touch the child's skin (or a door handle or other metal furniture) to equalize or discharge any static build-up before touching the child's implant components.

- Remove the speech processor and headset if you can't avoid activities or environments with extreme ESD. For example: plastic playing equipment (especially plastic slides), rooms filled with plastic balls, trampolines, plastic gym mats, plastic hats/ costumes, and balloon-filled rooms. Many families of young children avoid plastic play equipment altogether.

- Wear the cords next to the skin under clothing.

- Use anti-static treatments where possible.

  1. Antic-static rinses for hair, clothing.

  2. Staticide spray on carpets, car seats, drapes.

  3. Fabric softener sheets for wiping mats, furniture, screens.

4. Anti-static screens for small TV and older computer screen monitors.

5. Anti-static mats under CPU, mouse, and keyboard.

- Make it a rule that children cannot touch any TV or computer screens.

- Learn how to ground yourself. Teach your child — whenever she leaves the car — to ground herself by touching the car door as she touches the ground.

- Avoid synthetic materials and wool.

- Avoid trash can liners.

- Educate your child and all the people who play a part in your child's life about where ESD occurs and how to avoid it.

- Have a handout from the cochlear manufacturer's handbook to give to service providers, friends, and family. Add any information unique to your child and his situation.

MORE COCHLEAR IMPLANT PRECAUTIONS

- Make sure never to charge NON-rechargeable batteries.

- Throw out any batteries that look as if something is spilling out from them (the acid in the battery may be seeping out).

- Try AA Lithium batteries for lighter, longer lasting batteries.

- Always have a few copies of the patient identification card that comes with the device. You may need to show the card to avoid going through security detection. (You can also turn off the device, but the internal magnet will still cause the machine to beep.)

- Use a Medic Alert bracelet/wrist band that identifies your child as a cochlear implant wearer. You can have "NO MRI" (magnetic resonance imaging) put on the band, since this medical procedure is contraindicated for cochlear implant wearers. Also, electrosurgery in the area of the implant, electroconvulsive therapy, and ionizing radiation therapy cannot be used for CI wearers.

CHECKLIST FOR PROPER CARE OF THE COCHLEAR IMPLANT DEVICE

As with the hearing aids, routine inspection of the cochlear implant system will help to quickly identify any problems before they interfere with your child's learning. Optimal functioning can be achieved by routinely maintaining and checking the system, observing and giving appropriate responsibilities to your child. Here are some tips from parents and professionals.

Is the System Being Stored Safely When Not in Use?

TIP: Remove the batteries for long-term storage. Avoid skin contact with the batteries, however, as oils from the skin may interfere with battery longevity.

Are All Parts Of the System Getting Cleaned Regularly to Prevent Dirt Buildup?

TIP: Shake out any loose dirt, sand or dust if possible. Use a soft cloth and ask your audiologist how to wipe the external parts. Make sure all the parts air dry completely.

Clean the processor pouch by hand with damp cloth and mild detergent before airing out to dry.

TIP: Check the LED display screen and report any dirt or dust to your audiologist and/or manufacturer.

TIP: Check for accumulating dirt or dust in the transmitting coil (the part where there are grooves that the magnet screws into).

Is Any Excess Moisture Getting Into the Transmitting Coils or Speech Processor?

TIP: If you live in a humid environment or your child perspires heavily, you may need to use the dry pack supplied with the processor to remove excess moisture. Inspect the microphone ports but never clean out with water!

Are There Any Cracks or Frays in the Cables/Cords?

TIP: The short cord (headset cord) most commonly frays or breaks, because it is continually being pulled off and on. The long cord (transmitting cord), where it connects to the body worn processor, may get bent against the processor and eventually break. Also, any cord inserted into a part where there are prongs can make the prongs susceptible to bending and breaking.

TIP: Always have extra short cords on hand. Tuck the long cord under your child's clothing.

Are You Routinely Monitoring the Speech Processor With the Earphones Provided?

TIP: Connecting the monitor earphones to the speech processor's earphone socket allows you to hear the sound received by the microphone before it is processed. You can adjust the microphone sensitivity and volume to desired levels and identify any sound distortions.

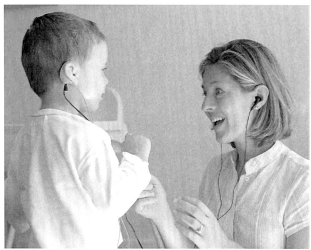

Checking the Cochlear Implant

Reprinted with permission from Cochlear Canada Inc.

TIP: Check the transmitting coil/headset with the signal check (wand) to check the integrity of the system (whether transmission through the cords between the headset and processor is working).

If the red light in the centre of the coil does not come on, start to eliminate the source of the problem by first changing the short cord, and then do the signal check again. If it still does not come on, then change the long cord. If the signal check light does not come on after this, then try using the lapel microphone instead of the ear-level microphone. Whether the light comes on or not at this point, you will need to contact your audiologist and manufacturer for support.

Are You Testing RF Transmission?

TIP: To check that the speech processor is sending sounds to the implant, turn on the processor and place the transmitting coil/headset over the back of the processor.

Are You Looking at the LCD Panel For Symbols That Indicate Malfunctioning?

TIP: The panel will show symbols that indicate a faulty program or low batteries. You may need to use another program, replace the batteries, or see your audiologist for more testing.

HELPING MY CHILD TO IDENTIFY AND PREVENT PROBLEMS WITH THE SYSTEM

- Does my child know that she must wear a hooded raincoat and waterproof clothing whenever the weather is wet or snowy? Have I cautioned her and her caregivers that her device is not waterproof?

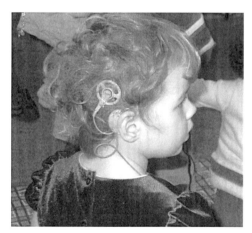

Tuck the cords under clothing

TIP: A young child can wear the processor in a sewn-in undershirt pocket to help prevent any water/liquid accidents.

- Is my child able to move freely and energetically without any parts of the device coming loose or falling away from her body?

- Am I encouraging my child to recognize any change in the functioning of his device and report any problems to an adult?

  TIP: Have an extra ear bud (earphone), signal-check wand, batteries and antistatic spray/wipes for daycare/school, so that your child can take some responsibility for problem solving.

  BONUS TIP: Keep a journal of your child's communication skills before and after cochlear implantation. See the appendix for an example of one parent's journal.

OBSERVING MY CHILD'S BEHAVIOUR

- Do I encourage my child to respond to the Ling 6 Sound Test on a daily basis at different distances to test for microphone and MAP functioning?

  TIP: Report any changes in your child's responses to your audiologist and other therapists involved!

  TIP: Include a "no-sound" turn when you are using the Ling 6 Sound Test ("ahh", "ee", "oo", "sh", "ss", and "m") to make it a 7-Sound Test. Make sure you vary the order of the sounds so that your child is not learning which sound comes next. Record the results of the test each day to trouble-shoot problems and measure progress over time.

- Do I observe my child's bahaviour, listening abilities, and speech quantity/quality/intensity changes to determine whether the device is faulty or a MAP adjustment may be necessary?

  TIP: Be aware of any changes in bahaviour (including taking off the device), the amount of support required to hear and pay attention to sound, and the amount of vocalizations or quality of vocalizations. Notice, too, his complaints about noise that requires you to alter the sensitivity setting by more than two levels. Also, note the presence of eye or facial twitch. **Any and all of these behaviours deserve immediate attention.**

ASSESSING THE ENVIRONMENT TO MAKE LEARNING OPTIMAL

- Is the background noise interfering with my child's experience of sound?

- Are sounds echoing off the walls, floor and windows?

  TIP: Rooms that are carpeted, have curtains, and have walls especially designed to absorb noise are best for your child's learning environment.

- Would my child benefit from a compatible personal FM system or Sound-Field FM system?

- Does the light source aid speech reading or cast shadows on the speaker's face?

- Is my child positioned to face the sound source — with her implanted side closest to the signal?

- Are my child's caregivers, teachers and peers informed about how to best support my child's listening and communicating development?

ASSISTIVE LISTENING DEVICES AND COCHLEAR IMPLANTS

Whether or not an assistive listening device is beneficial for cochlear implant users seems to be individual and

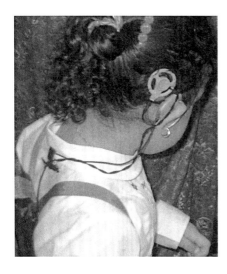

*Body worn
speech processor
back pack.*

may depend on other factors — such as the age of the
child's implantation and the acoustics of his environment.
Together with your audiologist and communication
specialist you can determine what FM equipment will be
beneficial and when to use it so that your child has equal
access to learning through spoken language.

A toteable sound system has reportedly worked very well
for school-aged cochlear implant users. This system is
similar to Sound-Field FM, but the loudspeaker is placed
on the child's desk and the teacher wears the transmitter
and microphone.

Children not using an ear-level processor may choose to
wear a personal FM system — if there are no problems
with interference.

Always refer to the FM manufacturer's instructions and
the cochlear implant manufacturer's directions about
using an FM with the implant to get correct information
about the equipment. Your audiologist and communication
specialist will help to evaluate the benefit of the FM at
different distances, in quiet and noise.

CHAPTER 8

BRINGING MY CHILD'S ATTENTION TO SOUND AND MAKING SOUND MEANINGFUL

How Can I Help My Child "Learn to Listen"? 109
Helping My Child Become More Aware Of Sound
    Information 110
What If My Child Is Deaf? 113
What If My Child Wears Hearing Aids? 113
Checklist of Listening Skills 115
Tracking My Child's Progress 119

HOW CAN I HELP MY CHILD "LEARN TO LISTEN"?

While wearing an appropriate hearing device consistently is the first step toward creating meaningful listening opportunities, children with hearing loss require specific experiences that will help them learn about sound.

- Paying attention to sounds and finding out **what** the sounds are and **where** they've come from are important activities for families with young deaf or hard of hearing children. Your child can then begin to learn about important sounds in his environment -to use that awareness to respond to a car horn, for example, or to speech sounds and spoken language.

I can bring my child's attention to sounds around him.

- When family members clearly and obviously react to everyday, naturally occurring sounds, deaf and hard of hearing children learn that those sounds have meaning.

- Besides the severity of the hearing loss and the degree to which a child benefits from hearing aid use, the chance that a deaf or hard of hearing child will learn spoken language also depends on **how much spoken language** — meaningful to the child — is used at home.

When you bring my attention to a sound and where it's coming from, I learn that sounds have meaning.

When I alert you to sounds, I'm teaching you to listen and make sense out of sounds.

Woof-woof.

By helping my child become more aware of sounds, I help him learn that sound has meaning.

HELPING MY CHILD BECOME MORE AWARE OF SOUND INFORMATION

Parents of deaf or hard of hearing babies, toddlers, and preschoolers can do some or all of the following to help their child learn to listen.

I can —

- Put the recommended hearing device on my baby during all of his waking hours.

- Alert my child to the sounds I anticipate hearing by saying, *"Listen!"* and pointing to my ear. Then, after hearing the sound, I can point to or name the sound source excitedly: *"I hear that!"*

- Get my child's attention to sound by calling his name, clapping, knocking, singing, and whispering.

- Imitate my child's own sounds (vocalizations, babbling, word attempts) and reinforce his speech: *"Good talking!"*

- Notice my child's detection and awareness of sound by paying close attention to his bahaviour when sounds are introduced. (He may blink his eyes, startle, cry, turn his head, smile, stop what he is doing, or vocalize — depending on his age and whether the sound is familiar or surprising.)

- Use a **clear, audible voice** and **be close** to my child when I speak to him. (It's best to be at the same level and within three feet of your child.)

- **Sing** my words and sentences. (A singing voice makes sound interesting and captures attention because of the intonation, varied pitch, rhythm, and intensity changes.)

- **Slow** my rate of speech slightly.

- **Pause** frequently. Expect my child to maintain listening attention by pausing before key, meaningful words.

- **Repeat** sounds and words to my baby for as many times as he is interested.

- Provide opportunities to play and see other children who use hearing aids and cochlear implants. (Being around other children with a hearing loss may help to make the connection between listening and a hearing device more meaningful.)

- Play with "noisy" toys such as musical instruments and other noisemakers I can control.

- Turn everyday routines and activities into "sound events." Make simple sound effects for noises and movements to label or describe the sound before and after I hear it. (For example, *"shhh"* goes the tap when you turn it on, *"brmmm"* goes the car, *"wheee"* when the child goes down the slide.)

- Read "noisy" books that talk about sounds and that have words describing sounds (*"crunch"* for stomping on autumn leaves, *"splish-splash"* for playing in the bath, *"rip"* for tearing paper).

- Have a bag of toy animals, vehicles, and other objects with sound associations. Bring the bag out and make one of the sound effects, such as *"shhh"* for the sleeping baby, or *"mmm"* for the ice cream cone. Take turns listening and repeating the sound before pulling out and showing the toy that matches the sound.

- Sort sounds by collecting small objects and pictures that begin with the same sound. Keep the items in a container labelled with the letter that makes that sound. Make a collage with the pictures.

The airplane goes-AHHH-ahhh-AHHH-ahhh.

WHAT IF MY CHILD IS DEAF?

It is initially important to stimulate the auditory nerve as much a possible through hearing aid amplification, and to evaluate what a baby with severe to profound hearing loss can detect and learn to hear. Using the strategies that help your child learn to listen is beneficial — whether your child continues to use hearing aids or becomes a cochlear implant user. Teaching your child as much as you can about sounds will prepare him to recognize and respond consistently to the sound (or sound-like sensation) he does detect. Over time, these reliable responses help to determine what he hears. If recommended, he will be better prepared for learning with a cochlear implant.

Therapeutic techniques — such as feeling the vibration of sound — develop an awareness of sound and clearly attach sound to meaning. You can still associate your child's experience of sound in this way by saying, *"Listen!"* and pointing to your ear (or his ear).

WHAT IF MY CHILD WEARS HEARING AIDS?

Every child is unique, and every child's hearing loss is also unique. How your child receives and perceives sound through his hearing aids may be different from another child with a similar hearing loss. In general, however, a child who is hard of hearing and uses hearing aids may not learn spoken language as part of his daily experience — the way a hearing child typically does. Speech sounds that have similar bands of energy are confusing and difficult to detect or discriminate. Normal conversation level may be barely audible and therefore require constant attention, concentration, and familiarity with the vocabulary. Sounds that are not emphasized or stressed in sentences (for instance: "the," "and," plural "-s," and the past tense "-ed,"or sounds at the ends of words) may be missed.

FOR ALL DEGREES OF HEARING LOSS

- Use the previously listed strategies for bringing your baby's attention to sound. Note: Most children can be "conditioned" or trained to respond to sound around two years of age for hearing testing. Working with your communication specialist and audiologist will ensure your toddler learns conditioned play audiometry appropriately and effectively.

- Emphasize the sounds that are easily confused. Ask for help interpreting the audiogram results in terms of what it means related to speech sounds.

- Always make sure the hearing device is working properly.

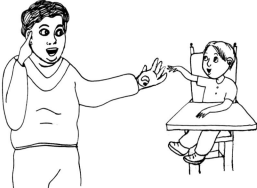

I can put appropriate, working hearing aids on my child.

- Encourage your preschooler to use strategies that help him to hear better. Model and describe good listening techniques — getting close to the speaker, moving to a quieter place away from background noise, advocating for himself by saying, *"I can't hear you; the music is too loud."*

- Give your child the opportunity to process information through listening alone — before adding the visual and tactile clues needed to develop confidence in his hearing and to strengthen his auditory skills.

CHECKLIST OF LISTENING SKILLS

What kinds of behaviour indicate your child is learning to listen? Consider the visual cues (other people's actions, body and facial expressions, or mouth movements) that your child may be responding to — instead of relying on his hearing. If you think there's a possibility that your child is reacting to what he is seeing — instead of what he is hearing — make a note of that on the following checklist. Then try to provide "listening only" opportunities and attach meaning to these experiences. Continue to use this checklist to help you choose the next listening goal.

Sound Awareness: When a child demonstrates an initial interest and response to sounds without necessarily knowing what the sound is, where it is, or what it means.

The skills below are listed in the order that they usually develop.

My child —

- Awakens to sudden noise and cries or is startled by sudden loud sounds.

     ____ All the time   ____ Sometimes   ____ Never

- Is soothed by voice.

     ____ All the time   ____ Sometimes   ____ Never

- Responds to sounds presented by the audiologist during hearing testing.

     ____ All the time   ____ Sometimes   ____ Never

- Changes his behaviour (becomes quiet or vocalizes) when hearing aids are on.

     ____ All the time   ____ Sometimes   ____ Never

- Responds when called.

     ____ All the time   ____ Sometimes   ____ Never

- Listens to conversation (watches speakers).

     ____ All the time   ____ Sometimes   ____ Never

- Responds to the word "no" (stops activity, turns to look, cries).

     ____ All the time   ____ Sometimes   ____ Never

- Tries to find out where sound is coming from.

     ____ All the time   ____ Sometimes   ____ Never

- Indicates when an ongoing sound stops (looks at the vacuum when I turn it off; stops dancing when the music stops).

- Conditions to sound (around 2 years of age) for hearing testing

     ____ All the time   ____ Sometimes   ____ Never

- Indicates when his hearing aids are off (either turned off, not working, or he's not wearing the aids) by pointing to his ears or the aids. This behaviour may not occur until later stages of listening skills.

     ____ All the time   ____ Sometimes   ____ Never

Discrimination: When a child demonstrates an ability to tell the difference between two or more sounds.

My child —

• Hears the difference between two familiar but different noises in the environment, such as the telephone and the vacuum. (Older children can communicate whether sounds are "same" or "different" after comparing the two sounds without seeing them.)

_____ All the time   _____ Sometimes   _____ Never

• Recognizes the difference between a few familiar, different sounding words (for instance, "boots" vs. "elephant"). Given two pictures or objects to choose from, he listens to the word you say, then points to one.

_____ All the time   _____ Sometimes   _____ Never

• Knows that speech sounds are not the same, based on the following characteristics of sounds:

The number of syllables (eg. "ba-by" versus "boy").

_____ All the time   _____ Sometimes   _____ Never

The length of sounds ("ah" versus "ahhhhhh")

_____ All the time   _____ Sometimes   _____ Never

The intensity (loud and soft sounds).

_____ All the time   _____ Sometimes   _____ Never

The different sounding vowels ("ahh" versus "ooo").

_____ All the time   _____ Sometimes   _____ Never

The different sounding consonants ("b" versus "m").

_____ All the time   _____ Sometimes   _____ Never

Identification and Comprehension: When a child demonstrates an understanding of sounds and knows what these sounds mean.

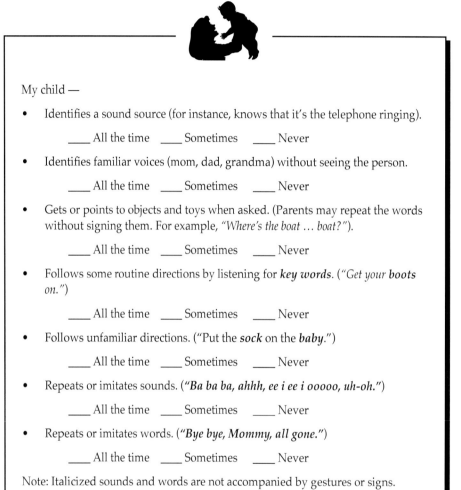

My child —

- Identifies a sound source (for instance, knows that it's the telephone ringing).

    ____ All the time   ____ Sometimes   ____ Never

- Identifies familiar voices (mom, dad, grandma) without seeing the person.

    ____ All the time   ____ Sometimes   ____ Never

- Gets or points to objects and toys when asked. (Parents may repeat the words without signing them. For example, *"Where's the boat ... boat?"*).

    ____ All the time   ____ Sometimes   ____ Never

- Follows some routine directions by listening for **key words**. (*"Get your **boots on**."*)

    ____ All the time   ____ Sometimes   ____ Never

- Follows unfamiliar directions. ("Put the ***sock*** on the ***baby***.")

    ____ All the time   ____ Sometimes   ____ Never

- Repeats or imitates sounds. (***"Ba ba ba, ahhh, ee i ee i ooooo, uh-oh."***)

    ____ All the time   ____ Sometimes   ____ Never

- Repeats or imitates words. (***"Bye bye, Mommy, all gone."***)

    ____ All the time   ____ Sometimes   ____ Never

Note: Italicized sounds and words are not accompanied by gestures or signs.

TRACKING MY CHILD'S PROGRESS

Sometimes parents find it easier to bring their child's attention to sound when they know what their child responds to and what they did to encourage his responses.

Here are several ways to keep track of your child's progress -

- Video recording

- Making notes

- Having another person observe your child

- Using a checklist

The following chart is an example of one way that you can record your notes. (Of course, your child's teacher or speech and language pathologist may suggest other methods.)

| Mon. | Dropped pot on floor. | Meg was startled. I said, *"Uh-oh, fall down, pot fall down."* |
| Wed. | Dog barking behind Meg. | Meg kept playing and seemed unaware. Bob pointed to the dog and turned her around to see it. |

I can keep a record of the sounds my child responds to.

Sound Events List

Here are some common sound associations:

SOUND	ASSOCIATION
Uh-oh	Something spills or falls down
Ahhhh	Airplane flying, opening mouth to look at throat
Ee -ee -ee	Mouse squeaking, monkey
OOooOOooOOoo	Fire truck
Shhhhh	Baby sleeping, water running
Sssss	Snake hissing
Mmmm	Eating something good
Hoo-hoo	Owl hooting
Ow	Getting hurt
Wheee	Going down the slide
Whoa	Slowing down, stopping
Yahoo!	Accomplishment
Yippee!	Riding a horse
Guh guh	Drinking
Kuhhhh (whispered)	TV or radio static
Caw caw	Crow cawing
High-yah!	Martial arts kick or punch into the air
Zzzzzz	Bees buzzing
Brmmmm brmmmm	Car driving
Rrrrrch! / screech!	Car stopping
Ahhh-choo!	Someone sneezing

DAY	SOUND EVENT What happened	OBSERVATIONS How did my child respond to the sound event? How did I respond to my child's response?

CHAPTER 9

OBSERVING MY CHILD'S COMMUNICATION

What Are the First Steps of Communication? 123
How My Child Uses His Body To Communicate 125
How My Child Uses His Voice To Communicate 126
Understanding What My Child Is Trying To
   Tell Me 127
Things to Look for During Home Routines 129
Things to Look for During Play Routines 131

WHAT ARE THE FIRST STEPS OF COMMUNICATION?

Parents of deaf and hard of hearing children eagerly wait for their child's first word (spoken or signed). But sometimes parents are not aware that children communicate messages long before they say or sign their first word. This early communication involves **sending, receiving,** and **exchanging messages.**

The development of this early **pre-language** communication **must** happen **before** a child can begin using "real" spoken or signed words.

Because pre-language behaviour can be very subtle, parents sometimes need to become aware of it and to respond in a way that is meaningful to the child.

When you show that you understand your child's subtle pre-language communication, he will feel successful and eager to communicate with you.

The following can assist you in learning to recognize those subtle cues which can help him to develop pre-language skills.

I can help develop my child's pre-language skills by —

- Recognizing how my child uses his **body** to communicate.

- Recognizing how my child uses his **voice** to communicate.

- Understanding what my child is trying to tell me.

- Responding in a way that encourages my child to continue in his efforts to communicate. (See *Chapter 10, Responding Positively to My Child's Attempts to Communicate.*)

HOW MY CHILD USES HIS BODY TO COMMUNICATE

To help you keep track of your child's development, we've listed several common methods he may use to communicate with his body. You can enter the date that you observe each action.

PRE-LANGUAGE

_____ **Eye gaze:** He looks at me, at an object, and back to me.

_____ **Entire body:** He shows positive and negative feelings by, for instance, using wild, jerky movements to show excitement.

_____ **Repetitive movements:** He repeats, again and again, a movement made with his hands, arms, or legs (repetitive movements may show early gesture or sign development).

_____ **Facial expression:** He smiles or frowns to show positive or negative feelings or his mouth forms an "O" to show surprise.

_____ **Hands:** He touches me to communicate and get my attention or to give or show me an object.

_____ **He gives a universally-understood gesture** like waving, pointing, or showing.

_____ **He moves his hands in the air** — not defined enough to be a real sign, but not so haphazard that it appears to be aimless.

TRUE LANGUAGE

_____ **Baby signs:** He uses an immature form of adult sign or invented signs. For instance, signing _"Mother"_ with one finger on face, instead of all five fingers; or he uses the correct number of fingers for _"father"_, but with the wrong placement on his head. (The sign for father then becomes more like the sign for deer.)

_____ **Signs single words** correctly.

_____ **Combines signs.**

HOW MY CHILD USES HIS VOICE TO COMMUNICATE

Often, when a child begins using his voice to get his message across, he will also continue using his body to communicate. This is normal and should be encouraged. Your child's use of his body to communicate will not prevent the development of spoken communication and may actually encourage more use of speech.

Again, to help you keep track, this checklist outlines several common methods he may use to communicate with his voice.

PRE-LANGUAGE

_____ Cries to express hunger, discomfort, etc.

_____ Gurgles or chuckles to express pleasure.

_____ Vocalizes (uses vowel, or vowel-and-consonant sound) in response to someone who is holding or playing with him.

_____ Babbles (repeats series of same sound — "bu, bu, bu").

_____ Babbles with voice moving up and down in pitch.

_____ Babbles with a variety of sounds (vowels, consonants).

_____ Jabbers in "sentences" (no real words).

TRUE LANGUAGE

_____ Approximates real words with sounds that always mean the same thing (for instance, says "ba" for "bottle").

_____ Says first real word.

_____ Begins combining words.

UNDERSTANDING WHAT MY CHILD IS TRYING TO TELL ME

Use this chart to help you understand why your child is communicating with you. Pay close attention to your child's message, so that you can respond in a way that encourages him to communicate.

When your child learns that you do understand, he will be more likely to try again. When you interpret what your child may be trying to communicate and then respond appropriately, he learns to communicate the same way again; because he was successful in getting his message across to you.

Why My Child Communicates

The following checklist can be used to chart your child's progress.

My child communicates to get his **needs met** when he wants me to —

____ Get him something.

____ Do something.

____ Stop doing something.

____ Take something away that he does not want.

My child communicates **to be social** when he —

____ Wants my attention.

____ Needs comforting.

____ Wants interaction with me.

____ Wants to play a game.

____ Wants to greet me.

My child communicates to **share his interests** when he **wants me to look at** —

____ An object.

____ Something that is happening.

My child communicates when he **wants me to comment about** —

____ An object.

____ Something that is happening or has already happened (for instance, spilled milk).

My child communicates when he **wants information from me** about —

____ An object (for example, a new toy).

____ Something happening (for instance, a sibling crying).

THINGS TO LOOK FOR DURING HOME ROUTINES

Mealtime

Watch how your child shows he is hungry or wants more food. How does he use his body or voice to communicate? Here are a few ways children communicate the messages *"hungry"* or *"more."*

Body: Smacks lips, looks towards food, reaches toward food, points, goes to parent and pulls her toward the refrigerator, climbs up and opens cupboard, signs *"more"* or *"eat."*

Voice: Cries, vocalizes (*"ah"*), babbles (*"bububu"*), tries to say a word such as *"mo"* for more or *"mu"* for milk.

When my child cries and looks toward the bottle, she is communicating to try to get her needs met.

Toileting

Is your child nearing the stage of toilet training? How does he let you know he has a dirty diaper or needs to go to the toilet? Here are typical ways children communicate this:

Body: Facial expressions (shows child is aware of dirty diaper or wet pants), points to or pulls off pants, holds self, signs a single word, such as *"pee," "poop," "diaper,"* or *"toilet."*

Voice: Cries, jabbers (no real words), *"uh-oh,"* or tries to say single words such as *"pee,"* or *"poop."*

Reaching and making sounds are both ways my child can communicate what he wants.

Bathtime

Does your child try to tell you something when he takes a bath? What about when you try to wash his hair? Watch what he does with his body and voice.

- When he wants you to get something, for instance, his duck.

  Body: Reaches and points.

  Voice: Cries. Says or signs *"duck."*

- When he **wants you to stop doing something**, for instance, washing hair.

  Body: Pushes your hands away.

  Voice: Cries or yells. Says or signs *"no."*

- When he wants **you to look at something**, for instance, soap bubbles.

  Body: Looks at the object (bubble), looks at you, looks at the bubble again, touches the bubble and looks at you again.

  Voice: While reaching for or pointing to the bubble and looking at you, he may say or sign *"bubble"* and smile at you.

THINGS TO LOOK FOR DURING PLAY ROUTINES

I can watch my child's communication during play.

Peek-a-Boo

Play a few rounds of peek-a-boo with a blanket and then pause. Does your child try to communicate to you that he wants the game to continue? How does he let you know? Does he —

- Look at you, then look at the blanket, then look at you expectantly?

- Pull the blanket over his head or push blanket toward you?

- Show sad expression to indicate displeasure that you've stopped?

- Try to say "boo" or use a facial expression that shows surprise?

Roll the Ball

Does your child try to let you know he wants his turn with the ball? Does he —

- Reach toward the ball?

- Look at the ball while hands and legs move with excitement?

- Try to form hands into shape of sign for ball?

- Try to say or sign the word "ball" or "more?"

CHAPTER 10

RESPONDING POSITIVELY TO MY CHILD'S ATTEMPTS TO COMMUNICATE

Advancing My Child's Self-Esteem 133
Encouraging My Child To Communicate
More Often 135
How Can I Respond Positively? 136

ADVANCING MY CHILD'S SELF-ESTEEM

A child's opinion of himself is built on how others react to him. He is sensitive to adult behaviour — whether an adult responds to him warmly or appears to be disinterested.

When we let our children know that we're trying to understand what they're telling us, they get the message that they are important.

Before your child begins using real words or signs, he may try to communicate with you in many other ways: eye contact, pointing, babbling. When you attempt to understand or interpret what he is trying to tell you, you're letting him know you care. This is like putting money into his (or her) bank of self-esteem.

Let's take one example: During bathtime, when a baby splashes water, he may watch for his mother's reaction. If she joins in his game by laughing, he'll get a positive message: You are worthwhile. You are important. I enjoy being with you.

When I let my child know I understand him — I send the message he is important and I care.

ENCOURAGING MY CHILD TO COMMUNICATE MORE OFTEN

- When you respond to your child's communication attempts, you're rewarding and helping him learn. He will feel successful and be encouraged to make more attempts to communicate with you. This increases his opportunities to practice new skills (new sounds, gestures, signs, facial expressions, or spoken words).

- If you ignore your child's attempts to communicate, he may become discouraged and then will make less effort to try.

- Sometimes, parents are so anxious about their child learning to talk that they expect — and only reply to — certain kinds of communication. For example, parents may ignore a child's babbling, because they are waiting for him to say a real word. Or parents may not recognize a child's facial expression or gestures as communication, because they're expecting true language.

- By recognizing and responding to the more subtle means of communication (a look, a gesture or action), you're helping your child develop skills that are the building blocks necessary for using a more sophisticated form of communication — sign language or spoken language.

- If you think you may be overlooking some forms of your child's communication, take a look at Chapter 9, Observing My Child's Communication.

HOW CAN I RESPOND POSITIVELY?

Before my child has "true language"

I can respond positively by —

- Looking at my child and smiling.

- Giving my child a gentle touch or pat.

- Nodding my head and pointing to what my child is trying to talk about (or picking up the object of discussion).

- Imitating my child's actions, facial expression, and body language.

- Imitating my child's sounds.

When my child is starting to use "true language,"

I can respond positively by —

- Imitating my child's words or signs.

- Saying or signing something back to my child about what I think he is trying to tell me (for instance, names of objects or activities).

- Complying with my child's request or explaining why I must say no.

Here are some examples of ways to respond positively to your child's early communication attempts (before he or she has "true language") —

Blowing Bubbles

Your child's eyes widen as she notices bubbles. She looks at you and then back at the bubbles again.

In addition to talking or signing, I can respond to my child's communication by smiling, nodding and imitating.

WHAT SHE MAY BE TRYING TO TELL YOU:	ONE POSITIVE WAY YOU CAN RESPOND:
Look, Mom! Bubbles!	Smile, nod and point while you say / sign, *"bubbles."*
*What **is** that?*	Imitate her questioning facial expression. Point to the bubbles and say / sign *"bubbles."* Then blow some more and again say / sign, *"bubbles."*
I'm afraid.	Smile reassuringly, pat her, and say / sign, *"You're scared. It's okay. A bubble. A nice bubble. Let's catch a bubble."*
More bubbles, please.	Imitate her excited facial expression. Say / sign, *"More. More bubbles. You want more bubbles."* Then blow some more bubbles.

Wind-Up Toy

Your child touches a car, but it does not move. He looks at you quizzically.

WHAT HE MAY BE TRYING TO TELL YOU:	ONE POSITIVE WAY YOU CAN RESPOND:
Help! Make this car move again.	Wait for eye contact. Then say / sign, *"Go car. You want car to go."* Next, push the car to demonstrate movement. Then, say / sign, *"Go car."* Then, wind up the toy and hand it back to your child.
(He pushes the toy car away and starts crawling off.) *I'm finished playing now.*	Say / sign, *"Finished! Clean up. Thank you."*

Playing Ball

You and your child are playing ball. Your child says, *"Ba! Ba!"*

WHAT SHE MAY BE TRYING TO TELL YOU:	ONE POSITIVE WAY YOU CAN RESPOND:
Hey, Mom, get ready to catch. I'm going to throw the ball to you.	Smile, pat her to let her know you are proud of her for saying this new sound. Imitate her sound, *"ba."* Then, say / sign, *"Ball. Ball. Okay, roll the ball."*
I like playing ball.	Smile and give her a hug. Say / sign, *"Ball fun. We're happy."*
That's my ball.	Smile and nod. *"Yes, your ball. Peggy's ball."* Then give her the ball.

I can respond positively to my child's communication, even if she is not yet using true language.

Playing With a Stuffed Animal

Your child sees her favourite stuffed kitty. She reaches and moves towards it, then flexes her fingers a few times.

WHAT SHE MAY BE TRYING TO TELL YOU:	ONE POSITIVE WAY YOU CAN RESPOND:
I want to play with that toy.	Smile. Say / sign, *"You want Kitty. Get the kitty."* Then, move the toy kitty closer to your child or give it to her.
(Now your child hugs the stuffed kitty.) *I love my kitty. It makes me happy.*	Smile. Say / sign, *"Happy girl. You love kitty. Here's kitty."* Then give the kitty a hug.

By watching my child I can guess what she is trying to tell me with her actions and sounds, then I can respond positively.

Now consider how you would respond positively to your child if he appears to be sending you messages like these —

At Bathtime —

WHAT HE MAY BE TRYING TO TELL ME:	ONE POSITIVE WAY I CAN RESPOND:
Oh! That's hot!	
Splash!	
I want my duck!	
Uh, oh! All wet.	

Changing Diapers —

WHAT HE MAY BE TRYING TO TELL ME:	ONE POSITIVE WAY I CAN RESPOND:
No! I don't want my diapers changed.	
Ooooh. Stinky.	
Glasses! I want Daddy's glasses! Pull off (as parent bends over child).	

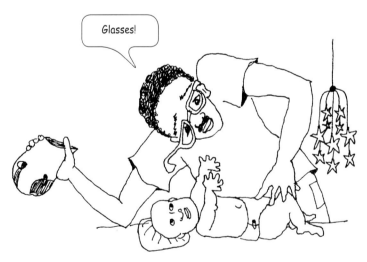

When I respond positively to my child's message I'm building his confidence and self-esteem.

Mealtime

WHAT HE MAY BE TRYING TO TELL ME:	ONE POSITIVE WAY I CAN RESPOND:
More! I want more.	
Down. I want down!	
Not carrot juice! I want milk.	

Responding positively to such messages gives your child a new feeling of confidence. He knows that you understand what he's trying to convey. More than anything else, this is the best way possible to advance your child's self-esteem.

CHAPTER 11

GETTING CLOSE TO COMMUNICATE

*Why Should I Get Close To Communicate
With My Child? 145
How Do I Get Close Up With My Child? 147
Checklist for Getting and Keeping
My Child's Attention 148*

*Communication improves
when my child and I
are face-to-face.*

WHY SHOULD I GET CLOSE TO COMMUNICATE WITH MY CHILD?

Getting close to your child is the first step in improving communication. Go through the following list to discover how close-up communication may work for you.

Close-Up Communication —

- Gets my baby's attention.

- Makes my voice louder in a noisy situation, giving my child a better chance at hearing speech sounds and understanding the message.

- Reminds me to follow my child's interests (see Chapter 15, Following My Child's Lead in Play and Interest).

I can bend down to my child's level.

- Helps my baby to get more information about what I'm saying from my facial expressions and movements.

- Makes my speech more easily heard by reducing the distance my voice has to travel.

- Creates "bonding" or "closeness" between my baby and me and develops his self-esteem by telling him that his communication efforts are worthwhile and important.

- Models good listening and shows how to pay attention.

- Encourages my child to tell me more.

HOW DO I GET CLOSE UP WITH MY CHILD?

Take time from a busy day to relax and to place yourself face-to-face with your child. Then see what happens to the quality of your communication.

Kneel, sit, lie, stoop, crouch or bend (watch your back!) down to your child's level.

A few soft cushions, mats or pillows on the floor may encourage family and friends to get down next to your child.

If your child is in a wheelchair or spends a lot of time sitting, make sure you have a comfortable chair at the same height as his chair to pull up beside him.

If your child is still a young baby, bring his level up to yours by having him near you in a high chair, on your lap, or in a side or front "baby sling".

From a parent:

"My son enjoys watching me work in the kitchen, so I put him in a high chair when he was young, and it made it easier for me to involve him in what I was doing. As he got older, we used a booster seat and then a step stool so he could reach the counter."

Getting face-to-face at storytime helps my child see me and the book more easily.

CHECKLIST FOR GETTING AND KEEPING MY CHILD'S ATTENTION

_____ Is my child's hearing device on and working properly?

_____ Are there auditory distractions — background noises such as TV, other conversations, dogs barking, baby crying, etc?

_____ Are there other auditory challenges — a room with no sound absorption, changes in his hearing loss, or otitis media? (See the Glossary of terms in Appendix D)

_____ Am I close to my child — within three feet and at the same level?

_____ Are there visual distractions — too many toys, moving objects, TV left on, etc?

_____ Are there other visual challenges — bright lighting, dim lighting, or a vision loss that requires being at an optimal distance within the visual field?

_____ Is my child hungry, unwell, or tired? Adjust expectations accordingly.

_____ Does my child associate sound with meaning? For example, what has my child learned about responding to his name being called?

I can point to things and keep objects near my face to get my child's visual attention.

CHECKLIST FOR GETTING AND KEEPING MY CHILD'S ATTENTION
(cont'd)

_____ Do I frequently provide a positive, meaningful consequence to paying attention and responding?

_____ Do I model paying attention by observing my child, noticing his attempts to communicate, and responding positively to his communication attempts (even if he is an infant and uses pre-language communication such as crying)?

_____ Am I trying techniques that make listening easy — using a sing-song voice, an animated expression, or visual props?

_____ Am I giving my child a chance to participate so that our communication is interactive, or am I doing all the talking?

_____ Am I pausing and expecting my child to have a turn at communicating?

_____ Am I offering my child appropriate choices whenever possible?

_____ Am I communicating at — or just one step above — my child's language level? (Refer to Chapter 16: Modifying the Length and Complexity of My Message.)

CHAPTER 12

USING APPROPRIATE INTENSITY AND RATE IN SPEECH

What Is Intensity? 151
Why Is Using Appropriate Intensity Important? 151
Things to Look for and Do 153
Why is Using Appropriate Rate of Speech Important? 154
How Do I Know If I'm Going at the Right Speed? 155

WHAT IS INTENSITY?

Intensity means the loudness or quietness of a sound.

WHY IS USING APPROPRIATE INTENSITY IMPORTANT?

- Appropriate intensity means using the right amount of loudness or quietness so your child can "hear" you to the best of his ability when he is wearing his hearing aids or cochlear implant.

- When you use appropriate intensity, you are helping your child learn more about speech.

- If you speak too loudly, your speech may sound "unnatural."

- If you speak too quietly, your child may not be able to hear you at all.

- Sometimes it is right to speak **LOUDLY**: for instance, when you need to get your child's attention **right now.**

- Sometimes it's right to speak quietly: when the baby is sleeping, or when using whispered speech to get attention, or to emphasize softer speech sounds. (But check to make sure your child can hear and understand you.)

My child hears me best when I use appropriate intensity.

It's important to watch for signals that tell me my voice is loud enough for my child to hear.

THINGS TO LOOK FOR AND DO

Use the suggestions that follow to help you achieve appropriate intensity whenever you talk with your child.

When I am talking with my child I always —

- Make sure that the hearing aids or cochlear implant are on and working.

- Use a normal conversational voice and change my intensity when it is appropriate.

- Keep background noise to a minimum. I turn off the TV, radio, noisy fans and other appliances if I can. (Rooms with carpets and drapes also help keep the noise level down.)

- When I am working with my child's communication specialist, I can ask about how to use techniques that highlight certain speech sounds by pairing certain consonants with certain vowels, whispering them, or emphasizing them to make them more audible.

My child will have trouble hearing what I am saying if there is a lot of background noise.

WHY IS USING APPROPRIATE RATE OF SPEECH IMPORTANT?

Rate means how fast or slowly you're talking.

- To help a young child learn language, people around him should speak clearly and at a normal, or just "slightly slower than typical" rate, without over-exaggerating.

- Your child will learn to imitate what he sees and hears.

- It takes a while for a child to process what he hears or sees. This means that he needs time to think and then try to understand before he can take a turn in the conversation.

If you use an appropriate rate of speech you are providing a good language-learning model for your child and giving him the gift of time to process the language.

The Gift of Time

HOW DO I KNOW IF I'M GOING AT THE RIGHT SPEED?

People naturally use a rate of speech that is comfortable for them. Some people always speak quickly, and others always speak more slowly. Many people speak more quickly when they feel anxious or stressed. They may speak more slowly when they're trying to emphasize what they're saying, or when they are speaking to someone who has little understanding of the language.

When people speak to young children they almost automatically talk a bit more slowly. This is a feature of "motherese" or "child-directed speech," the language that

Speaking at an appropriate rate helps my child understand me better.

mothers and fathers use when they talk to their children. Even very young children will naturally use this slightly slower way of talking when they speak with a child younger than themselves.

Note: It is much more common for parents to speak too quickly rather than too slowly. If you think you might be a fast talker it will be important for you to learn to slow down a bit. Adults with a hearing loss often say they find it very difficult to follow a conversation when someone speaks too quickly — running words together.

It's not always easy to recognize it when your own rate of speech is inappropriate (too fast or MUCH TOO slow). You're more likely to notice it when someone else is speaking too quickly or too slowly. If you are not sure whether your rate of speech is appropriate, you can —

- **Ask** someone else for their feedback.

- **Video or Audio-tape record** and listen to myself.

- **Observe** my child's response to see how much of what I'm saying he understands.

Speaking too fast makes it hard for my child to understand me.

- **Listen** to my child's rate of speech. If he is speaking too quickly or too slowly, he may be imitating me.

- Ask my communication specialist about how to use techniques that emphasize target sounds appropriately. For example, if our goal sound is **"k,"** it may be appropriate to slow down those words that have the **"k"** sound. You can even repeat the sound at the beginning of words such as "It's a **k-k-kite.**"

I can help other people learn to talk at an appropriate rate.

CHAPTER 13

USING EXPRESSION TO ENCOURAGE COMMUNICATION

Why Is This Goal Important? 159
How To Make Faces 160
How To Make Your Body Talk 163

WHY IS THIS GOAL IMPORTANT?

Facial expressions and body language are a very powerful means of communication. They can make communication clearer by:

- Emphasizing a spoken or signed message.

- Adding more information to the spoken or signed message.

- Taking the place of spoken words or signs.

Using facial expressions and body language helps my child to understand what I'm saying and how I'm feeling.

We know that —

- Visual information such as facial expressions can be so powerful that when the auditory communication (what we hear) and visual communication (the expression we see on someone's face) is contradictory, we tend to pay more attention to the visual message.

- When we speak, we change the intonation in our voice to add meaning to our message. Young deaf and hard of hearing children may have more difficulty hearing these intonation changes, so we can add visual information for them by making our faces more expressive.

- We can keep a baby's attention longer if we are more expressive with our faces — and if we use gestures.

- Young children communicate using facial expression and body language long before they say or sign their first word (see Chapter 9 — Observing My Child's Communication).

It is very important for parents of young deaf and hard of hearing children to be aware of their use of facial and body expressions and to understand how to successfully use these communication tools to build their child's developing language skills.

HOW TO MAKE FACES

Adults, like children, are all unique individuals who have their own likes, dislikes, strengths and weaknesses. With that in mind, it's easy to understand that not everyone feels comfortable using facial expressions. If you are one of those people who has trouble "making faces," keep in mind how important it is for your child's communication development to use as many facial expressions as possible.

Here are some ideas. Try one or two that sound as if they might work for you.

- Start using facial expressions when you and your child are alone together. No one else will see you, and no one else will tell. When using facial expressions feels more comfortable and natural to you, you'll find it easy to "make faces" whenever you're talking with your child.

- Use a mirror to see how you look as you make faces that show different feelings. Start with happy, sad, excited, surprised, angry and tired. Move on to looking puzzled, disappointed, curious, bored and hungry. (Hint: If you put a mirror up in a place where you often talk with your child — beside the change table or highchair, for instance — you'll have many opportunities to see the faces you both make throughout the day.)

- Play "facial charades" with other family members. Make a face and see if the others can guess what feeling you are trying to express. This gives you a chance to "read" others' facial expressions, too.

- Record yourself if you can get a video or movie camera. Then later sit back and watch. See how you're doing with the faces you're making. Are they —

  1. Clear and expressive?

  2. Appropriate for the situation?

  3. Not too fast?

  4. In your child's visual range?

- Record again in a few weeks to see your progress.

- Point out the facial expressions of characters in picture books and try to imitate them.

- Use a little humour and imagination as your child becomes increasingly aware of facial expressions and what they mean. Exaggerate or use a wrong expression on purpose. Watch your child's reaction and encourage him to laugh along with you.

- Watch how the "experts" do it. If you can, take in some live theatre. As you enjoy the production, try to focus on how the actors move and use their bodies to convey their message. If you ever have the opportunity to see a deaf theatre troupe perform, be prepared for a lively production filled with energetic body language. Any time you communicate with deaf or hard of hearing adults, you will see firsthand the powerful way in which they use body expressions.

- You can also watch video tapes of deaf adults telling stories. Ask your community library for help in obtaining such tapes.

HOW TO MAKE YOUR BODY TALK

Like *"making faces,"* body language offers a powerful tool for helping you communicate with your deaf or hard of hearing child.

You probably already use a lot of body language, naturally, when you communicate. Becoming more aware of the way you use your body is a big step in using body expressions appropriately. Consider the following words and the natural gestures that go with them:

hi	darn!	stop!	hooray!
bye	no	give	
yes	ouch	go	
shhh!	come	wait	

Play body charades with other family members. Use just one part of your body to show words or phrases.

USE YOUR FEET AND LEGS TO SHOW:	USE YOUR HANDS TO SHOW:	USE YOUR FINGER TO SHOW:
fast	delighted	come
slow	angry	wait
tired	hungry	no
climbing	big	itching
walking in mud	small	listening
walking in water	mine	thinking
walking in snow	cold	over here
being quiet	playing with a ball	right there
feeling angry	using the phone	wanting a cookie
feeling excited	peeling a banana	using a computer
feeling shy	wanting something up high	
needing to go to the bathroom		

Using more facial and body expressions is a natural way to limit unnecessary directions and questions. You'll find yourself making more comments and acknowledging your child's ideas. This is a good strategy for helping your child's language and self-esteem grow. (For more information about using comments and questions, see Chapter 18.)

CHAPTER 14

DECIDING TO USE SIGNS

The Goal *165*
Ways of Communicating With Deaf and Hard of Hearing Children *165*
Which Approach Is Right for Us? *170*
My Concerns About Using Signs *174*
What Should I Start Signing *175*
How Do I Learn Signs or Other Visual Communication Systems? *176*

THE GOAL

When a family's language used in the home is a spoken language (not signed), the goal is often for the baby with the hearing loss to use what hearing she has and learn to talk. The family will then use special techniques that stimulate spoken language development to strengthen the baby's listening skills. Other families may supplement spoken language in some way — with signs and/or picture communication systems — when that approach is recommended to accelerate language development.

WAYS OF COMMUNICATING WITH DEAF AND HARD OF HEARING CHILDREN

You are following the hearing specialists' (audiologist, ENT) advice and your baby is using an appropriate hearing device during all of his waking hours. If you are also using the sound awareness and communication strategies explained in the previous chapters in this book, you have already begun promoting your baby's spoken language development. You may be wondering about which method of delivering language to your baby is best. It is important to learn as much as you can about the different approaches. Then choose what you feel is best

— based on what you know about your baby's needs, what your specialists recommend, and what you observe works well.

Your communication choices reflect your communication goals. For example, you may talk with your child while her cochlear implant device is on to meet the goal of using speech and hearing to communicate. You may also choose to learn some signs that may be helpful when the device is off — for instance, when she is taking swimming lessons. Basically, families choose to communicate by speaking, signing, or some combination of both. (See Appendix F: Learning to Listen and Communicate from a Child's Point of View to read about one family's choice and their now seventeen year old daughter's view of her life.)

Auditory-Verbal and Auditory-Oral Methods

The most common approaches to using only spoken language with deaf or hard of hearing children are the Auditory-Verbal and Auditory-Oral methods. These communication methods require sufficient hearing across speech frequencies (the different pitches that make up speech sounds). Hearing aids, cochlear implants, and assistive listening devices are used and early intervention is focused on auditory stimulation and making sounds audible and meaningful. Family involvement is vital for the child to learn about listening and speech during daily spoken language experiences. Both approaches emphasize developing spoken language through listening. An Auditory-Verbal (A-V) approach to developing spoken language emphasizes strengthening the auditory channel through listening only — before any visual information is presented. The child learns to develop confidence in her hearing — initially, under ideal conditions when the speech or sound signal is easily detected and interesting to the child. The Auditory-Oral method also incorporates visual cues such as speech reading.

Cued Speech

The Cued Speech method requires the speaker to use handshapes near the mouth to cue the listener to confusing sounds (such as "g" versus "k", or "m" versus "p"). Typically it takes parents about six months to learn the cues and to use them while talking.

Sign Language

Sign Language is a true language. Sign Languages are different all over the world. North Americans use American Sign Language. People who know American Sign Language (ASL) do not necessarily know Chinese Sign Language. American Sign Language is a recognized, real language that has its own rules and endless possibilities, just like any other language. It is better known as ASL and is part of what defines the Deaf as a cultural group.

It is possible to communicate anything in ASL that can be communicated in English. ASL is not a form of English. In ASL, words are not represented in English word order. ASL has many unique characteristics and language rules that are not present in English. Body language and facial expressions are important features of ASL. Because ASL is independent of English, it is not possible to speak English and sign ASL at the same time.

Manually Coded English

Manually Coded English (MCE) is a visual representation of the English language. It is not a true visual language, but just a way of showing English with your hands. The signs may be borrowed from ASL, but some are invented or altered to reflect the English letter that begins the signed word.

Hearing parents may choose MCE, because it allows them to express themselves visually in their own language. Parents with children who gradually lose their hearing or have acquired hearing loss may use MCE to retain English.

Sign-Supported Speech and Language

Using ASL signs in **English word order** to visually represent some parts of spoken language is often employed when parents are first trying to use signs, rather than ASL word order. Research indicates that using signs to support speech and language does not hinder communication development and may stimulate spoken language development. Many children benefit from visual language support, especially when a hearing device isn't used consistently, or when there are concerns about progress. Although advanced diagnostic procedures make it possible to diagnose newborn babies with hearing loss, there are also children who are not diagnosed in infancy and may be significantly delayed in speech and language development. When there is an increased risk of a significant language delay for a toddler or preschooler who has just been identified as having a hearing loss, parents may support spoken-word development with signs during a period when their child is accumulating quality hearing experiences and learning to listen. Children who have age-appropriate language skills but delayed speech may use signs to avoid frustration.

Signs that support spoken language development are often a "bridge" to completely oral communication, or are used as a "back-up" in certain situations — in difficult listening environments (noisy) and when the hearing device is not in use.

When there is an increased risk of a significant language delay for a toddler or preschooler who has only recently been identified as having a hearing loss — or one who is facing additional learning challenges — parents may support spoken-word development with signs, while evaluating their child's unique learning abilities, progress, and the benefit he gets from amplification. Children may also make themselves understood and avoid frustration by using signs to support their own unclear speech.

Parents may learn ASL from a fluent sign-language instructor, and then incorporate those signs into visually supporting the spoken language they use with their young child. Sign-supported speech is an approach used at the BC Family Hearing Resource Centre when there is evidence that using signs to complement spoken language is advantageous for the child's development and when there are concerns about progress, using only spoken language approaches, over a reasonable period of time.

OTHER RELATED TERMS

Bilingual/Bicultural Approach

The Bilingual/Bicultural approach to education promotes the use of American Sign Language as the main language of instruction at school. English is usually taught as a second language through reading and writing. Along with learning both languages, children learn to appreciate and respect the culture and traditions of those people using sign language and those who use spoken language.

Conceptually Accurate Signed English (CASE)

This system combines the English word order with ASL signs that depict the concepts you are are talking about.

Simultaneous Communication

The term Simultaneous Communication means that speech and signs are used at the same time.

Total Communication

Total Communication is a philosophy of communication that encourages the use of whatever communication system is necessary for the child to be a successful communicator. It may include a combination of speech, speech reading, sign language, fingerspelling and listening.

WHICH APPROACH IS RIGHT FOR US?

Parents of a child who has been diagnosed with a hearing loss often feel confused and unsure about how to communicate with their child. It's okay and extremely common to worry and wonder whether the communication method you choose is the "right" one. In fact, if you're frequently evaluating how your child is learning to communicate — and in what ways he's best able to communicate — then you have the advantage of making appropriate decisions for your child according to his current learning abilities — which may vary over time.

Different developmental stages of communicating can be described as pre-language and true language and as nonverbal and verbal. All young children begin to communicate by using pre-language forms.

If your child is an infant, newly diagnosed, or if he has additional needs, he may be using many pre-language forms of communication.

Pre-language forms of communication typically occur before true language forms. They are important for establishing early communication that resembles conversation.

For example: Your child **reaches, cries** or **looks** at an object; then you respond by picking him up, feeding him, or giving him the object. When you respond to his pre-language message (reaching, crying or looking), you reinforce his attempt to communicate. By responding **immediately**, you have encouraged your child to try to communicate again in the same way — especially if he got what he wanted.

Talking and signing are examples of true language. True language communication develops the ability to communicate abstract, unique and creative ideas.

If your child is older and other children his age have started to communicate with real words (signed or spoken), it is essential for him to learn a form of true language communication. Signs may help to keep the "language centres" of the brain stimulated and provide a more advanced form of communication needed for healthy language development.

Typically, hearing children start to use true language — spoken words — between their first and second years of life. By then, they will have heard many examples of true language spoken by others around them and have practiced communicating with pre-language forms — pointing, reaching and babbling (baby talk).

Check Which of the Following Ways You and Your Child Communicate.

	PRE-LANGUAGE	TRUE LANGUAGE
VERBAL	____ Crying ____ Single sound babbling (says one sound or syllable such as "guh" or "oh") ____ Repeated sound babbling (such as "da-da-da" or "um-um") ____ Combined sound babbling (child combines a variety of sounds such as "uh-buh," or "bee-doo")	____ Talking
NONVERBAL	____ Eye contact ____ Reaching and pointing ____ Using facial and body expression ____ Gesturing	____ Signing

Note: If your child is between age eighteen months and two years and has no true language, you may want to consider adding signs to spoken words.

Children who have some degree of visual impairment and hearing loss may require a tactile (touching) form of sign language in addition to vision and listening training. If your child has other challenges (mental or physical), you may want to consider how he learns best and whether he is physically able to coordinate speech or sign movements.

Whether you child will learn more effectively through speech, sign, or a combination of speech and sign depends on facts that are unique to each child and family. Some families choose to emphasize both sign language and speech because they want their child to have the opportunity to communicate in a variety of ways in order to achieve his maximum potential. Often signs act as a bridge to speech and can help to "jump start" spoken language.

You may have questions or concerns about sign language that are best discussed with others who have experience communicating with deaf and hard of hearing individuals. For example, deaf or hard of hearing adults, teachers of the deaf and hard of hearing, speech-language pathologists, audiologists and parents of deaf or hard of hearing children. If you think you may want to add signs to communicate with your child, you will need information and support from professionals, family and friends.

For help in answering some of your questions about hearing loss and using sign language, see the list of useful information in Appendix A: Helpful Resources.

MY CONCERNS ABOUT USING SIGNS

There could be many reasons why you may be unsure about using signs with your deaf or hard of hearing child.

- I'm not sure about using signs to communicate with my child because I don't know any signs, and I'm afraid I can't learn them.

- Using signs would mean that my child can't really hear.

- No one in my community uses signs, so who else will communicate with my child?

- I'm embarrassed to use signs around others. People will stare at us and think we're different.

- My child won't learn to listen and talk if we use signs.

Many families wonder if using signs will discourage their child from listening and talking as quickly and as well as he can. There is no evidence that proves this one way or the other. In general, spoken language stimulates listening and speech when combined with appropriate hearing device use. Signs may complement language development when recommended.

Some families have discovered that using signs, in addition to emphasizing speech and listening, got communication going — until eventually they dropped the signs altogether. Some families continue to use sign language and spoken language separately in different situations — until they are comfortable using either. If your child is not using a hearing device during all of his waking hours or is not making expected progress, then signs or other communication systems may be necessary.

WHAT SHOULD I START SIGNING?

If you're wondering what to start signing, it's helpful to know **what your child wants to communicate.**

Young children typically want to talk/sign about:

- What they want, feel or need. For example: *Want juice. Pretty ball. Ow, hurts.*

- Who is important to them — or interesting to look at. For example: Daddy or Mommy are **important**. A kitty or a baby is **interesting to look at.**

- The whereabouts of something or someone. For example: *Mommy, where? Where shoe?*

- When something or someone is gone. For example: *Apple all gone. No hat on. Mommy bye bye.*

- When something happens repeatedly or something reappears. For example: *More piggyback! Peek-a-boo!*

- When something belongs to someone. For example: *My bear. Baby's rattle.*

To summarize: words and ideas that are appropriate to sign for a young child are those that describe what he's interested in — the people in his life and what he needs (or needs to do). Signs for words like these are also important: *where, no, all gone, more, mine and yours.*

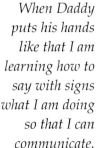

When Daddy puts his hands like that I am learning how to say with signs what I am doing so that I can communicate.

"Off."

Use This Chart to Pick the Words That Are Important for You to Sign With Your Child

	WORDS TO SIGN WITH MY CHILD
What does my child often **want**?	
What is my child **interested** in (objects)?	
How is my child **feeling**?	
Who is **important** to my child?	
What is my child thinking when we look for **something** or **someone**?	
What is my child thinking when we make something happen again, and what are the **games we play over and over?**	
How does my child know that something **belongs** to **someone**?	
Other thoughts that my child wants to communicate.	

HOW DO I LEARN SIGNS OR OTHER VISUAL COMMUNICATION SYSTEMS?

The communication specialist working with you may provide more information about where to learn sign language, or she may make a referral to another specialist who has expertise in that area. It is important when learning signs to study, if possible, with a teacher who uses sign fluently — ideally a deaf or hard of hearing adult. There are many excellent resources available for learning signs from a video, DVD, or interactive software program. It is helpful to refer to a sign language dictionary once you have learned some signs. Find more information about using signs from the organizations and websites listed in Appendix A: Helpful Resources at the end of this book.

PART II: BECOMING PARTNERS

In the previous chapters you have been focusing on learning new ways to make what you say / sign to your child more easily available to him.

Now that you've started learning how you can better communicate with your deaf or hard of hearing child, you and your child are ready to learn together how to be communication partners. By focusing on your child's interests, adjusting your message to his level of understanding, taking turns, and using comments more than directions or questions, you'll both enjoy the beginning of real conversation.

Chapter 15: Following My Child's Lead in Play and Interest …179

Chapter 16: Modifying the Length and Complexity of My Message …187

Chapter 17: Encouraging Turn-Taking …199

Chapter 18: Questions, Commands and Commenting …205

Chapter 19: Modelling Specific Sounds, Words, and Sentence Formations …219

FOLLOWING MY CHILD'S LEAD IN PLAY AND INTEREST

How to Follow 179
Why Follow My Child? 180
How Is It Going? 181
Directing Play and Conversation 183

> Splash!

When I follow my child's lead I am sending her the message that what she says and does is important.

HOW TO FOLLOW

- **Watch** your child. Pay attention to his nonverbal behaviour (actions, facial and body expressions, and where he is directing his attention). Consider what he may be thinking or feeling.

- **Observe** which events or objects he is noticing, playing with, or experiencing.

- **Match** your words/signs to your child's experience.

WHY FOLLOW MY CHILD?

(Instead, shouldn't I be teaching him the words I think are important?)

Too often, adults try to direct a child's attention to what they think is important. But, researchers who study **how** children acquire language have discovered that learning is most effective when an adult's words/signs are specifically related to the child's interests or needs.

Here are some of the reasons —

- A child can more easily learn the meaning of new words when he can **link** words/signs to what he is seeing, feeling, hearing, doing.

- He is more likely to **imitate, voluntarily,** our words/signs.

- He will usually remain in a conversation with us for a longer period of time.

- He gains self-confidence and builds a positive sense of self-esteem.

Following your child's lead takes practice. Most adults, by habit, try to direct a child's attention to what they have planned for him or what they are interested in.

It helps to sit back and take the time to "read" your child's behaviour so you have a better idea of what he is thinking or feeling. Then you can better use the signs or words that match what he may want to say.

From a parent:

*"Following my child's lead was quite difficult for me at first. I felt I should be directly **teaching** him. My child's deafness wasn't diagnosed until he was almost two. I thought I was wasting time when I just **followed his lead** rather than **teaching** him something specific. But I started relaxing when I realized it really does work. My son was more likely to learn new words when I was talking about something he was focused on."*

HOW IS IT GOING?

Parents of deaf and hard of hearing children often feel an urgency to "make every second count" when they're playing with their child. For this reason, many get into the habit of directing much of their child's play, because they want him to learn. Habits are often hard to change. Some parents have said that learning to follow their child's lead was a difficult strategy for them at first.

Pay close attention to your own actions when you play with your child. Do you find yourself trying to guide him towards specific toys or actions? Do you try to change his play activity before he is ready? Or do you allow him to continue with an activity that he finds enjoyable? (Try not to urge a change simply because you've become bored.)

HINT: We're sometimes more directive than we think we are. Ask a friend or partner to watch while you play with your child. He or she can use the following chart to record when you direct the play in some way and when you let your child determine what happens. Then, take a look at the chart. Are you satisfied with the interaction? If not, try working on this the next time you're playing with your child. Try to **increase** the number of times you let your child guide the direction of the play and **decrease** the number of times you take charge. But don't be too hard on yourself. It may take several weeks to learn this way of playing with your child.

I DIRECTED MY CHILD'S PLAY	I FOLLOWED MY CHILD'S LEAD
Examples:	Examples:
_____	_____
_____	_____
_____	_____
_____	_____
_____	_____
_____	_____
_____	_____
_____	_____
_____	_____
_____	_____
_____	_____
_____	_____
While Brian put the newspaper on his head, I talked about the toy truck on the floor.	Brian put the newspaper on his head, and I talked about his _"hat."_
Sally said: _"Dolly crying."_ I didn't follow her play acting. Instead, I started my own story. I picked up a toy tiger and said, _"The tiger is big."_	Sally said: _"Dolly crying."_ I followed her play acting and answered, _"Your dolly's crying. She's hungry."_

DIRECTING PLAY AND CONVERSATION

Here are two examples of a parent talking with his child. In the first example, the parent is trying to direct the child's play and conversation. In the second example, the parent is following the child's lead.

SARA	FATHER
Sara is pulling hard, trying to remove her sock.	*"Look, Sara. Put the block on."*
"Uh!" Sara continues struggling with her sock.	*"Come here, Sara."*
Sara, ignoring her father, smiles as she successfully pulls off sock.	*"Look! Blocks! Put the block on."*

In this above example, the topic of the father's conversation did not match what Sara's interests were at the moment. So Sara missed the opportunity to learn new words/signs, because she and her father were not sharing the same experience.

Now, see what might happen when Sara's father **follows her lead.**

SARA	FATHER
Sara is pulling hard to remove her sock.	Dad leaves tower of blocks and sits down near Sara.
"Uh!" Sara continues struggling to remove her sock.	*"Sock off! Pull sock off, Sara."* *"Stuck! Uh-oh. Pull sock off!"*
Sara looks up at Dad, then looks at her sock and again looks at Dad.	*"Off! You want sock off!"*
Sara successfully pulls her sock off, looks at Dad and smiles. If she is ready, she may even try to sign/say a word such as *"off."*	*"Yeah! Off! Sock off. You did it!"*

From a parent:

*"At first it was very hard following Ying-ying's lead. I **so much** wanted her to talk that I was constantly trying to direct her to do or say things. But following her lead finally paid off. I sure was surprised to discover that Ying-ying tried to say new words more often when I followed her lead than when I tried to **make** her say something. We also had more fun."*

Now Sara and her father are paying attention to the same event or object. Sara's father is interpreting what Sara may be thinking and feeling. He's using words or signs that Sara may want to express. This time Sara is given words/signs that **match** what she is experiencing. This makes it easier for Sara to learn the meaning of new words, and increases the likelihood that she will imitate one of her father's words or signs.

Following your child's lead is a very important skill to learn.

Remember, when you follow your child's lead —

- He knows you're paying attention.

- You're sending him the message that what he says and does is important.

- He is more likely to learn the meaning of new words and may voluntarily imitate your words or signs.

- He has greater opportunities to learn new language, because he is more likely to stay with you — for a longer period of time — in a conversation that interests him.

CHAPTER 16

MODIFYING THE LENGTH AND COMPLEXITY OF MY MESSAGE

Learning Language: Why Is It So Difficult? 187
Why Modify My Message? 190
How Can I Modify the Length of My Message? 192
How Can I Modify the Complexity of My Message? 196

Communicating is like playing on a team: we make adjustments so that everyone can participate.

LEARNING LANGUAGE: WHY IS IT SO DIFFICULT?

Imagine yourself in a room full of people who are speaking German, Spanish, Cantonese, or any other language you don't understand. You are kept there for three weeks — eating, sleeping, and playing among people speaking foreign languages.

By the end of the first week, you understand a few words; but (depending on the situation, gestures and tone of voice) you're still mostly guessing what others are saying. It helps when someone **points to an object and repeats the same word again and again** so that you learn what it means.

By the second week, you've learned the names of most of the daily routines: lunch, bedtime, bathroom. You can understand a brief sentence like "I'm tired." Or "Good food." But you have a difficult time expressing yourself with more than one word.

Even at the end of three weeks, you can pick out only a few **key** words from a conversation. It's very frustrating, because you still have to communicate mostly through gestures and pointing. When someone finally sits down with you and — **using only one or two words — comments on what you're doing, thinking or feeling**, it's a great relief. You're grateful to this person who shows patience and who also makes an effort to modify his message to your level of understanding.

In the beginning I can help my child begin to learn language by using 1 or 2 words at a time.

Now, think about your child, who may be experiencing even greater communication challenges while he's learning your language. His hearing loss may leave him with fewer clues. If your child has a profound hearing loss, it may be extremely difficult for him to guess what it means when you move your mouth around.

Remember, you have already mastered your first language. Unlike you, your child does not have any knowledge about language.

Even with some residual hearing and hearing aid use, many of the sounds your deaf child may hear will sound the same or similar (particularly if he has not learned to distinguish the differences between sounds). Possibly, you and your child will hear the same sounds differently — especially if your child has a sensorineural (inner ear) hearing loss, which causes sound distortion.

Let's go back to that room full of foreign speakers. When a friend you've made there tries to show you the difference between the words "big" and "little," he uses his hands to gesture as he says the words. This helps, because your ears are not yet "tuned" to recognize unfamiliar sounds as

being different from each other. For example, the words that mean "big" and "small" in another language may sound almost identical to you. This is the reason why some Japanese say "rike" for "like" when they are speaking English. In Japanese, the English sounds "r" and "l" are interchangeable and sound the same to the Japanese ear.

So when you're first learning language, you need to keep seeing hand gestures for words like "big" and "small" — until you become familiar with the differences between the words. Finally, you begin to think of the word that means "big" as sounding a certain way and the word that means "small" as sounding slightly different.

Of course, those children who have better hearing will also have a better chance at "cracking the code." Since they get more information about sounds, they are better able to tell the difference between sounds.

If your child is having a difficult time listening in order to communicate, adding sign language may help him develop the language and thinking skills necessary for learning to listen. **Your child may be able to make more sense of sounds once he can associate each sound with a sign.**

To summarize: If you want your child to understand what you're communicating, it's essential to adjust your message to meet your child's level of understanding.

WHY MODIFY MY MESSAGE?

You probably already know what kinds of messages get the best results when communicating with young children. Which of the following two instructions will Johnny, a two year old, be more likely to understand?

Parent: *"Well, I guess we better put all this stuff back, because I have to take Ginny to the doctor and then pick up the pictures over at the supermarket. Okay?"*

Parent: *"Johnny, clean-up time!"*

The first message gives Johnny information about why he needs to clean up and what activities will follow. However, you probably identified the second message as more effective and to the point. In the second message, the parent gets Johnny's attention and then clearly tells him what is expected.

Let's look at this from your child's point of view. When you modify your language to his level of communicating, he understands your message. Equally important, he will think positively about his own attempt to communicate.

Less like this ...

More like this ...

Here is what he learns —

- **You can understand me.**

- **I can understand you.**

- **I can take my turn.**

- **I can use ways of communicating — instead of inappropriate behaviour — to get what I want or need.**

HOW CAN I MODIFY THE LENGTH OF MY MESSAGE?

If I want my child to understand what I'm communicating, I can modify my message to suit my child's level of understanding.

No expert tennis player, teaching a beginner, would ever hit the ball as hard as possible — or hit it into the far corners of the court. In the same way, you won't want to use long sentences when your child still has only one word — or no words — to communicate. A good tennis instructor hits the ball slowly, straight to her student at first. For the beginning player to improve, the instructor must use skills that are only slightly above the beginner's level.

I can adjust the number of words and/or signs that I use so that my language is only one step above my child's level.

Similarly, if your child is going to attempt to build sentences, he needs to hear and/or see words that are only a little beyond his current stage of language learning. By modifying the number of words and/or signs you use, you should try always to be just one step above your child's level, helping him up to your level.

Record your child's language level every few weeks or months, and modify your message length to match.

Here are some examples and a chart for you to use.

IF YOUR CHILD SAYS/ SIGNS:	THEN YOU SAY/SIGN:	EXAMPLE:
No words	Single sounds and one word.	**Child:** (Holding ball) **Adult:** *"Ba, ba . . . ball."*
One word	Two words	**Child:** *"Ball."* **Adult:** *"Big ball!"*

MY RECORD

DATE	MY CHILD SAYS/SIGNS	I SAY/SIGN

HOW CAN I MODIFY THE COMPLEXITY OF MY MESSAGE?

AT FIRST I CAN —	MESSAGE TO MODIFY	MODIFIED MESSAGE
Just give the **key word** in my message:	*"Where are your shoes?"*	*"Shoes?"*
Repeat ... repeat ... repeat... my message.	*"Shoes on."*	*"Shoes on."* (Wait for child to start putting shoes on.) *"Shoes on."* While child puts shoes on, say: *"Shoes on."*
Simplify my intended message.	*"Take off your shoes and put them in the laundry."*	*"Shoes in laundry."* Or, *"Shoes off. In laundry."*
Give choices in my message.	*"What kind of sandwich do you want?"*	*"Want peanut butter or tuna?"*
Break the message down into parts.	*"You need to get the stool and wash your hands before eating your snack."*	*"Get the stool for the sink."* *"Wash your hands, all clean."* *"OK. Now snack time."*
Add **facial and body expressions, gestures, and signs** to my message.	*"Where is your bottle?"*	*"Where is your bottle?"* Sign and say the word bottle while looking around quizzically. Then point to the cupboard where the bottle is.
Try to say the **same message in different ways.**	*"Good night"*	*"Night-night. Sleeptime. Bedtime."*

LATER ON I CAN —	MESSAGE TO MODIFY	BETTER MESSAGE
Rephrase my message to include more familiar words.	*"Tidy up the knick-knacks above your dresser."*	*"Put the toys on your dresser away."*
Elaborate on my message to provide more information.	*"Put on your shirt."*	*"Put on your red shirt."*
Break my message down into **parts or steps.**	*"Set the table."*	*"Here are the placemats. Get four forks and four knives. Set four places at the table."*
Give **feedback** to my child during my message by nodding my head, smiling, and repeating necessary information.		*"Pick up your clothes and put them in the laundry."* (My child picks up his clothes.) *"Yes, put them in the laundry."*

If your child faces additional challenges, you can still follow the same formula for modifying your message. He may go through the learning stages more slowly, or may stay at one stage for a very long time; but continue to communicate at his level of understanding.

CHAPTER 17

ENCOURAGING TURN-TAKING

Why is Turn-Taking Important? 199
How to Encourage Turn-Taking 199
Strategies for Encouraging Turn-Taking 202
How To Recognize When Your Child Is Taking
   A Turn 203

WHY IS TURN-TAKING IMPORTANT?

When people talk together they take turns talking. So, conversations are a series of turns in talking. This ability to take turns has been found to be a very important skill necessary for early communication development.

Turn taking in conversations should be somewhat like a tennis or ping-pong game. To keep the ball going, each person must take a turn hitting the ball back to his partner. To keep a conversation going both partners need to take turns talking, and the number of turns taken by the partners needs to be balanced. When parents are interacting with their child, the parent and the child should be both initiating and responding. In this chapter you will learn ways to encourage turn-taking in your own child.

HOW TO ENCOURAGE TURN-TAKING

Early on, you can encourage your baby to take **nonverbal** turns. If your baby is encouraged to imitate your actions, you are showing him to take a turn after you do something. For instance, take a spoon and hit it on your baby's high chair table. Give your baby a spoon and encourage him to imitate this action. Then encourage your baby to take turns playing this game by handing the spoon back and forth to each other. You can also say *"My turn!"*

From a parent:

"It seemed so hard at first, but encouraging Jimmy to take turns really paid off. It's so much more fun to talk and play with him now, and it's great to see him able join in on games with his friends or his brothers."

Your turn!

I can encourage my baby to take turns.

when you take the spoon and *"Your turn!"* when you give him the spoon. You can play other games that encourage imitation and turn-taking actions like Peek-a-Boo or Clapping Hands. Many babies and toddlers enjoy pushing and pulling toys. You can encourage turn-taking with toys so that you watch and copy what each does with the toy. When you talk as you take your turn, you are preparing your baby to take a turn after you have **said** something.

After your baby is able to imitate your actions, you can move on to conversational, or **verbal**, turn-taking. You will want to encourage a back-and-forth turn-taking in conversations with your child. You can start by watching for your child to communicate in some way. Take a turn by responding positively (see Chapter 10), and then signal to your child that it is his turn again. You can signal to your child by waiting, smiling, and looking at him with anticipation. More turns and longer conversations provide your child with increased opportunities for learning speech and language.

Adults sometimes neglect to give a young child enough time to take his turn. Be patient. Children often need a longer wait time than we might expect.

*I can pause and wait to give my child
the opportunity to take a turn.*

If you are concerned that your child is not yet taking turns, spend some time observing yourself in play and communication with your child. Sometimes when parents are feeling anxious that their child is not yet talking, they will do things that they think will help their child learn to talk. Instead, they actually end up discouraging conversational turn-taking. For instance, parents may ask their child lots of questions — "What's this? What's that?" Or they may try to direct everything the child is doing during playtime. Here's a checklist that may help you to see if you're using strategies that encourage your child to take turns in conversations.

STRATEGIES FOR ENCOURAGING TURN-TAKING

___ I play turn-taking games - pushing a ball or car back and forth, playing patty cake, blowing kisses, taking turns playing following the leader, making animal sounds such as "ba-ba" or "moo moo."

___ I engage in activities that my child really enjoys, so he will want to take more turns in the interaction.

___ I keep my own turns short, but fun and interesting, so that my child does not lose interest before it's time for him to take a turn.

___ I pause and wait long enough to give my child time to take a turn.

___ I signal my child that it is his turn by looking at him with anticipation, by pointing or gesturing (for instance, holding out my hands to catch the ball), or by saying or signing "your turn."

___ I follow my child's interest, rather than trying to control the play.

___ I use actions, sounds and words or signs that are within my child's ability to imitate or use.

___ I make comments, rather than ask a lot of questions or give directions.

___ When my child stops interacting, I try to keep him with me by encouraging him to take one more turn to extend the interaction or conversation before finishing.

Patty cake. Patty cake.

HOW TO RECOGNIZE WHEN YOUR CHILD IS TAKING A TURN

Sometimes adults fail to notice when a young child does take a turn, especially if the adults consider only speech or signs as a "real" turn. It will be important for you to learn to recognize when your child is taking his communication turn, so that you can respond. Sometimes a child's early communication turn can be quite subtle. (See Chapter 9: Observing My Child's Communication Skills.)

From a parent:

"Our routine includes my saying and signing, 'I love you,' and Jeffrey saying and signing the same thing to me."

Infant Turn-Taking

Very young babies often show turn-taking in a conversation in these ways:

- Gazing at a partner

- Smiling

- Blinking

- Sucking or stopping sucking

Babies can even show that they want turn-taking to stop by:

- Looking away from the partner

- Crying or looking displeased

- Falling asleep

Next stages of Turn-Taking

As your child develops, he may begin taking turns by:

- Vocalizing

- Taking your hand

- Behaving in ways to get attention — throwing toys, for instance.

- Looking

- Imitating your actions, gestures, sounds

- Pointing

- Nodding

- Creating her own message through sounds, gestures, words and sentences

As you can see, turn-taking, or two-way communication, is a significant stepping stone in your child's speech and language development. It's important to help your child develop this skill early on. If you become concerned because your child is still not developing turn-taking skills, you may want to talk with a communication specialist to determine if a thorough communication assessment is recommended.

CHAPTER 18

QUESTIONS, COMMANDS AND COMMENTING

Why Should I Limit Unnecessary Questions and
  Commands? 205
Helpful Ways To Talk With Young Children 206
Limiting the Use of Questions When I Already
  Know the Answer 207
Limiting the Use of Questions That Can Be Answered
  With One Word. 208
Limiting the Use of Commands or Directions to the Times
  When I Really Want My Child To Do Something 208
Using Commenting 209
Using Commenting: A Brief Summary 212
Some Examples of Good Language-Learning
  Conversation 213
How Am I Doing? 215

WHY SHOULD I LIMIT UNNECESSARY QUESTIONS AND COMMANDS?

Adults often ask lots of questions in conversations, but young children learn language best when adults limit their use of question.

As adults, when we meet a new friend, we often engage in a conversation that is full of questions. Usually, when we ask another adult a question, we are asking for information that we do not already know.

We also ask lots of questions when we're talking with young children. Sometimes these questions are necessary (*"Where did you put your hearing aids? Please tell Mommy."*) But many times we ask questions that relate to information that we already know. **So, are we helping young children learn to have conversations when we ask them lots of questions? Probably not!**

Parents of very young children will initially use helpful methods of talking. (For instance, making comments such as, *"Oh, Manisha wants her juice."*) As a parent becomes concerned or frustrated when a child does not begin talking or signing, the parent may get into the habit of asking many more questions and increasing his or her directions or commands.

Sometimes parents are much more directive and controlling with their deaf and hard of hearing child than with the hearing sisters and brothers, because they think this will help with language growth. Unfortunately, the opposite is true.

HELPFUL WAYS TO TALK WITH YOUNG CHILDREN

Here is a short list of helpful ways to talk with young children. (This is explained in further detail on the following pages.)

When my child is first learning language, I help best when I —

- Limit the use of questions when I already know the answer.

- Limit the use of questions that can be answered with one word.

- Limit the use of commands or directions to the times when I really want my child to do something.

- Use commenting.

LIMITING THE USE OF QUESTIONS WHEN I ALREADY KNOW THE ANSWER

Children are often more reluctant to talk when they feel they are being **tested** or **pressured** to perform.

Here are a few examples of questions where we might already know the answer —

"What's that?"

"What colour is that?"

"What's that called?"

"What's this?"

"Is that a ball?"

"Who's that?"

What's this?
What's that?

Too many questions may make my child reluctant to talk.

Use **what/where/who/what colour** questions when you really **do** want the answer. For instance, *"What do you want for lunch?"*

LIMITING THE USE OF QUESTIONS THAT CAN BE ANSWERED WITH ONE WORD

Questions that can be answered with a single word seem to **stop** or **block** conversations from proceeding. A child may lose the opportunity to practice saying a longer sentence or to take more turns in a conversation.

Here are some examples of questions that can be answered with one word — these kinds of questions may **not** be helpful.

> *"What colour is it?"*
>
> *"Do you want a cookie?"*
>
> *"Do you like kitties?"*
>
> *"Is that a ball?"*
>
> *"Did the bubble pop?"*
>
> *"Is that your puppy?"*

LIMITING THE USE OF COMMANDS OR DIRECTIONS TO THE TIMES WHEN I REALLY WANT MY CHILD TO DO SOMETHING

Avoid using a command or direction when you're trying to help your child learn new words or signs. It's appropriate to use commands and directions during routine activities — when you tell your child to *"get your shoes"* if you're going for a walk. Or to *"clean up now"* when playtime is finished. But we should limit commands that are used to direct a child's play or conversation. Here are some examples.

From a parent:
"I never realized how many questions I asked my child. I felt asking questions showed me how much he knew — his colours, names of things. But when I saw that he never really contributed what he thought to a conversation, my husband and I decided to rethink how we talked to him. The fewer questions we asked — and the more commenting we used — the more Chi-ming talked with us about what he was thinking and doing. It was amazing to us. But when you think about it, who wants to just answer questions all day?"

When you want to help your child learn new words during play or conversation, you can —

USE LESS OF THIS	USE MORE OF THIS
"Show me the cow. Put the cow there."	*"That's a cow. Cow says mooo. The cow is eating."*
"Put the big block on top" — when used as a way to direct a child's actions, rather than to make a comment about what a child has already done.	*"Wow! You put the big block on top.* *One, two blocks. Blocks fall down."*

USING COMMENTING

Observe your child's nonverbal behaviour to find out what interests him. Then build your comments around those interests. Talk about what your child is doing, noticing, thinking, or feeling. For instance —

> *"A **big** dog. Dog is barking. The dog scared you."*

> *"You are using blue. You are making circles. **Big** circles. You like to colour."*

You can also comment about what **you** are doing, thinking, or feeling. This, too, is a way of modelling language, speech and / or signs for a child.

> *"I'm eating soup. Yummm. I like it. I'm hungry."*

Commenting allows a child to hear words, see signs and understand that language is worthwhile and fun without having him feel pressured to imitate or respond on command.

When we make comments, children may respond by imitating us, which gives them wonderful language practice.

When we make comments, we are showing our children how to have conversations. They learn to respond to comments made by a conversational partner — not just in response to questions.

Young children learn to talk by being talked *with* rather than talked *to*. Many years ago the advice given to parents of young deaf or hard of hearing children was to "talk, talk, talk." However, parents were not given specific ideas about the best kind of talking. They were not cautioned to also "listen, watch, and take turns" with their language-learning children. We now know that young children learn best when parents talk about what their child is **seeing, thinking, feeling and doing.**

I can comment by talking about what my child is thinking, doing, and feeling.

Here are examples of comments parents might make to children at various language levels.

BEGINNING LANGUAGE LEARNER	INTERMEDIATE CONVERSATIONS	MORE ADVANCED PARTNERS
"Dog."	*"Dog is barking."*	*"That big dog is barking loudly!"*
"Cry."	*"You are crying."*	*"You are crying because Mary hit you!"*
"New shoes!"	*"You have new shoes."*	*"You have beautiful, shiny, new shoes."*
"Bubble popped!"	*"The big bubble popped!"*	*"The bubble popped in your eye, and that bubble soap stings."*

New shoes!

Commenting helps my child learn language.

USING COMMENTING: A BRIEF SUMMARY

Keep your talk at — or just above — your child's language level.

If your child is at the one-word stage, use two or three words when you comment. If your child uses four- or five-word phrases, you can use five to seven words.

Be sure you are talking about what interests your child.

If your child is not interested in what you are doing, talk about what your child is doing, thinking, and feeling. When your child watches as you do something, be sure to talk about what you're doing, thinking, and feeling, so that there are words to match the action your child sees.

Be sure your child is taking a turn in the conversation.

Use commenting when it is your turn in a conversation. Soon your child will also use commenting in conversations with you. In the meantime, encourage him to take turns using actions, words, signs, gestures, or vocalizations.

Be sure to continue to use lots of expression in your voice and your body language.

When you concentrate on using commenting, it's easy to forget to keep your voice and body interesting. Remember, if you look and sound flat or dull, your child will soon lose interest in what you're saying.

SOME EXAMPLES OF GOOD LANGUAGE-LEARNING CONVERSATION

In this first conversation, Dad doesn't direct or question. Alysa joins in the conversation on her own.

ALYSA	DAD (SIGNS/SAYS)
Points to cow in the picture, and looks at Dad.	*"Cow. A big cow."*
Puts her hand up near her forehead, and tries to say and sign *"cow."*	*"Yes! Cow! The cow says moo."*

In this next example, Grandma uses commenting to model for Ronny.

Ronny takes his turn with actions, vocalizations, and eye contact.

RONNY	GRANDMA
Hits the high chair tray with his spoon and says, *"Uh."*	Points to Ronny and says, *"Hungry. You are hungry."*
Says, *"Uh,"* kicking the bottom of the highchair.	Says, *"Cheese. Here's some cheese."*
Picks up cheese and puts in his mouth.	Says, *"Eat cheese. Yummy, eat the cheese."*
Looks at Grandma and says, *"Uh!"*	Says, *"More. More cheese. You want more."*

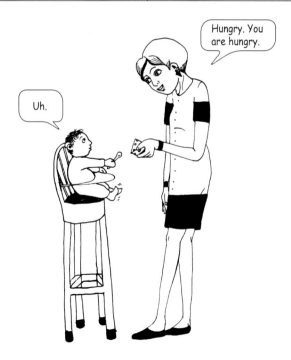

HOW AM I DOING?

As you go about your day, try to pay attention to **how** you're talking with your child. Are you asking lots of questions, or are you making comments?

Sometimes, we think we are making a **comment** just because we are **not** using **questions** like these: **what, who,** and **why**. Do you sometimes raise your voice at the end of a sentence: *"Nice kitty?"* Do you raise your eyebrows at the same time to communicate a question? For early language learning, even an implied question like this is less helpful than commenting.

Next, find out how often what you say to your child consists of commands. You may be surprised! In our busy everyday lives we often spend a large part of our day giving commands to our children. *"Get your shoes. Sit down. Brush your teeth. Put your jacket on."* Many of these commands are necessary at the moment. But there are other times when we can replace commands with comments.

As you do your chores or play with your child, you are **directing** your child to do something when you say: *"Throw the ball. Pop the bubble. Pour the milk in the bowl."* You can change these into comments by waiting for your child to do something and **then** making a comment about what your child just did. You will find your child is much more likely to imitate your **comments** than your **commands**.

It might be helpful to pretend you're a newspaper reporter. As a reporter, you're not allowed to interfere with the news event that is happening before your eyes. Instead, you must sit back and merely report or comment on what is happening.

HINT: Sometimes it's difficult to become aware of how you're communicating with your child. If you have a

tape/CD recorder (audio) or video/DVD camera, tape
a conversation between you and your child. Then count
how many times you're making **comments** and how
often you're using **commands** or **directions**. If you don't
have the equipment for recording your conversations,
ask a friend or partner to sit and listen to one of your
conversations. They can use a chart similar to the one that
follows to record the ways you're communicating.

If your chart shows twice as many **comments** as
commands or **questions**, you're doing well. If your chart
shows **questions** and **commands** make up more than half
of your conversation, you'll want to focus on **commenting**
more often whenever you play and talk with your child.

COMMENTS	QUESTIONS	COMMANDS

For deaf and hard of hearing children who have additional challenges — and for those children with very limited language — it's tempting for adults to ask lots of questions that don't require the child to contribute to the conversation. But even if a child has limited ability with language, it is important for parents to use more comments than questions. Commenting encourages children to develop and grow in their use and understanding of language and conversational skills.

If your child is not yet using real words or signs, he can still participate in the conversation. He may take a turn with a body movement or gesture or facial expressions to convey his thoughts and feelings and to indicate your turn in the conversation.

During your turn you can **say what you think your child might want to say** about what's happening and about his feelings. Watch his body language for feedback to let you know if you are matching his thoughts and feelings correctly.

CHAPTER 19

MODELLING SPECIFIC SOUNDS, WORDS, AND SENTENCE FORMATIONS

What Is Modelling? 219
Why Is It Important to Model Specific Sounds, Words and
    Sentences? 220
What Sounds Do I Model? 222
Speech and Language Milestones 225
What Are the Do's and Don'ts of Modelling? 229
Modelling Correct Speech and Words (Signed
    or Spoken) 230
Why Is My Child Making Mistakes? 232

Modelling is showing my child how to communicate

WHAT IS MODELLING?

Modelling is **showing**. It means that you provide your child with an example of how to communicate. As a parent, you are your child's most impressive model. Here are some examples of modelling —

- You show your child how to stir the icing for a cake and then let your child stir the icing.

- Your child says, *"ba, ba, ba"* (reaching for a ball) and you say, *"ball, ball, ball"* to show what he wants.

- You sign, *"stop"* to your child (when another child keeps tickling him, for instance) to show him what to do instead of hitting.

- You let your child watch you sitting quietly for the dentist to show your child how you want **him** to sit still for the dentist.

Up! Up!

Ah ah ah

I can model how to communicate by interpreting my child's communication attempts.

WHY IS IT IMPORTANT TO MODEL SPECIFIC SOUNDS, WORDS, AND SENTENCES?

There are many good reasons for you to use correct sounds and words with your child. Every time you use language around your child, you give him the opportunity to hear and see speech and signs the way they are supposed to sound and look.

Children learn about language and how to use it by observing the people around them who are already communicating. Modelling is especially important for children who are deaf or hard of hearing or who have additional needs; because they depend on clear, frequent examples to show them how to communicate.

Modelling helps my child if he -

- **Uses the incorrect sound, word, or sentence formation** (spoken or signed).

  Examples:

  "Um" for *"up."*

  "Tat" for *"cat."*

  "Me want up" for *"I want up."*

  "What you are doing?" for *"What are you doing?"*

- **Babbles** a string of sounds.

- **Makes random movements** resembling gestures or signs.

- **Does not use some sounds, words, or sentence forms** that other children around the same age or communication level are using. (Refer to the developmental checklist and your SLP or teacher to see which sounds and words are next for your child to learn.)

  Examples:

  She doesn't say the *"k"* sound.

  He says the *"s"* sound but doesn't say the *"sh"* sound yet.

  She says *"ahhhh,"* but not *"eeee."*

He signs *"mommy,"* but not *"daddy."*

She doesn't use the past tense verb form — *ed*, as in *"walked."*

He doesn't match the verb with the pronoun — as in *"He go,"* instead of *"He goes."*

I can model what I think my baby might want to say.

WHAT SOUNDS DO I MODEL?

Speech sounds, vocabulary, and language forms that your child is trying to make — or isn't yet making — are the most important to model.

Deaf and hard of hearing children need to learn sounds and language in roughly the same order of acquisition as hearing children. Hearing children typically learn these sounds and words without being taught. It is important for parents and caregivers of children with hearing loss to be aware of the usual speech and language development milestones. A child with a hearing loss may not develop speech sounds and language simply by overhearing conversations. For this reason, establishing appropriate speech and language goals — working together with your communication specialist — is essential for having realistic expectations and for remembering what is important for you to model.

Parents of deaf and hard of hearing children find it helpful to refer to a list showing the natural order in which children learn to say sounds and to use language. This is called a developmental list of speech sounds and language skills. (Note: even hearing children do not learn **all** the sounds, words, and language forms in **exactly** the same order.)

Deaf and hard of hearing infants will often babble or make vocal sounds. It's important to respond and imitate the same sounds back to your young child so that he's encouraged to continue vocalizing. If he says ,*"ahh,"* you could respond with a slight variation such as, *"ah ah ah."* The key is to listen to what your child says. Then, **repeat it back to him.**

When you repeat what you think your child is trying to say, you provide a useful model. For example, when he says, *"uh uh"* while lying in the crib, you might say, *"up up."* Pick him up while you say, *"up"* — so he learns that what he said has meaning.

Later on, your child may need more reminders about using his voice. Vowels *(a, e, i, o, u)* have a lot of sound energy and are the easiest speech sounds to hear. If your child is not vocalizing yet — or is producing only a few vowel sounds — use a variety of words with vowel sounds when you speak to him. Important vowel sounds to establish are *"ahhh"* — then *"ooo"* and *"eee."*

When your child vocalizes easily, you'll want to continue modelling those vowel sounds he isn't yet making. Add some consonant sounds as well. For instance: *"uh oh"*, *"hi"*, and, *"Baa,"* says the lamb, *"Ee-ee, ee-ee,"* says the mouse,

"Mooo," says the cow.

Once your child can produce these sounds, he only has to make some slight adjustments to form many other vowel sounds. The first consonant sounds to model are *"b," "m," "w,"* and *"p."* The consonant sound *"f"* may be easier than some other sounds for deaf and hard of hearing children to learn. The reason: That sound is easier to see (on lips) and to feel.

If your child is starting to make these beginning sounds, then he's probably also combining some of these sounds. Your child may learn to use additional sounds if you make sound combinations that he is not yet making. For example, if your child says, *"muh"* and *"ooo,"* you could try combining them to say, *"moo."*

SPEECH AND LANGUAGE MILESTONES

A Developmental Checklist for Getting Started with Modelling Sounds, Words, and Sentences.

Here are some of the skills that indicate speech and language development. The stages gives you an idea of approximately the kinds of sounds and words to model according to your child's hearing age. Together with the communication specialist (for example, speech-language pathologist or educator of the deaf and hard of hearing), you will choose goals like these based on formal and informal communication assessments. You will then learn ways to help your baby, toddler, or preschooler reach these goals. Since speech and spoken-language progress is related to hearing and listening abilities, it is important always to ensure proper hearing device use and model good listening first!

	SPEECH DEVELOPMENT	LANGUAGE DEVELOPMENT
THE FIRST STAGE: TAKING IN SOUND AND LANGUAGE *(first 12 months of hearing)* NOTE: During the first year, speech development follows quality hearing experience (full-time hearing device use). It takes approximately a year of optimal hearing experience as a foundation for true language to develop, and modelling good listening skills is critical at this stage. See the Checklist for Listening Development in Chapter 8 for more information on hearing milestones.	___ Babbles many vowel and consonant sounds ___ Babbles speech patterns: Intonation and inflection, numbers of repetitions of the same sound or word, or number of syllables in a word, and duration of sounds such as *ahhhhhhhh* versus *uh-uh-uh* ___ Uses a variety of pitches and loudness levels	___ Shows interest in objects ___ Responds to your presence and the sensations you provide: your voice, touch, smell ___ Intentionally (purposefully) smiles, frowns, reaches, or vocalizes in response to something interesting ___ Initiates behaviours in anticipation, such as reaching up when you approach ___ Attaches meaning to sounds (associates sounds and words with pictures, objects, events, and movements) shown by understanding some routine phrases such as *Mommy's home, Book time, Night-night, All gone.*

	SPEECH DEVELOPMENT	LANGUAGE DEVELOPMENT

THE SECOND STAGE: TWO-WAY COMMUNICATION
 	
 (between 12 and 24 months of hearing)
 	
 NOTE: syllables are the number of vowel sounds you can hear pronounced in a word. Different combinations of consonants and vowels in a word make up the word's shape. Examples of different word shapes are: *"me,"* where the consonant *m* and the vowel *e* make a consonant-vowel word-shape, *"up"* where the vowel *u* and the consonant *p* make a vowel-consonant word-shape, and *"pot,"* where the consonant *p*, the vowel *o* and the consonant *t* make a consonant-vowel-consonant word shape. It is important for babies to babble a variety of nonsense word shapes before putting consonants and vowel sounds together to make real words.
	___ Imitates the "Ling 6 Sounds": *ah, oo, ee, m, sh, s* (not necessarily all at once)
	
	 ___ Uses speech sounds: *p, b, m, n, w, h*
	
	 ___ Uses a variety of syllable and word shapes (see note)
		___ Uses at least ten words or word approximations to name objects and ask for things.
		
		 ___ Vocabulary rapidly increases
		
		 ___ Uses mostly nouns (people, common objects, places) and some verbs (action words such as *eat, sleep, play*) at first
		
		 ___ Uses a few pronouns, such as *you, me*
		
		 ___ Beginning to use more adjectives (descriptive words such as *big, red, fast, hot*) and prepositions (location words such as *in, under, behind*)
		
		 ___ Understands the difference between similar sounding words that may be confused during play, such as:
		
		     off versus *on*
		     car versus *cat*
		     baby versus *bye-bye*
		     cake versus *cookie*
		     hot versus *pot*
		     push versus *pull*
		     hop versus *stop*
		
		 ___ Follows simple directions
		
		 ___ Points to pictures
		
		 ___ Makes requests for *more* or asks *again*
		
		 ___ Uses at least 50 words intelligibly and combines two words together

	SPEECH DEVELOPMENT	**LANGUAGE DEVELOPMENT**
THE THIRD YEAR: COMMUNICATION BUILDING *(between 24 and 36 months of hearing)*	___ Adds speech sounds: *t, d, k, f, g, sh, s, ch, y,* and *j* ___ Understands the difference between single sounds that have been associated with meaning, such as the Ling 6 Sounds ___ Understands and uses words with: • The same consonants but different vowels *(boot, bat, bite, bait, beet, boat)* • The same vowels, but different consonant production, such as *moo,* (consonant is produced nasally) versus *boo* (consonant is produced orally), or *out* versus *ouch* (consonants are produced differently, but have similar tongue placement behind the front teeth) • The same vowels, but consonants that only differ in voicing (vocal cord vibration), such as *bus* versus *buzz* • The same vowels but different consonant placement, such as *shoe* versus *Sue* (both consonants are produced the same way but require slightly different tongue configuration) ___ Speech is understood by familiar listeners most of the time	___ Asks: *who, where, what* at first. Then, later *why, when, how* ___ Uses *want, need,* and *have* in phrases such as, *I want more, You have money, Sister needs shoes on* ___ Uses plural *-s* and possessive *'s* markers to show more than one *(cats)* and belonging *(Mommy's book)* ___ Understands negatives *no, not, don't* ___ Adds verb form *-ing,* such as *sleeping, running, hiding* ___ Uses subjective pronouns: *I, you, he, she, they, we* ___ Uses objective pronouns: *him, her, me, us, them* ___ Uses conjunction words, such as *and,* to join two sentences together ___ Uses possessive pronouns: *his, her, our, their, my, your* ___ Answers with *because* and *so* to give reasons ___ Understands and uses words to show amount *(some, any, none, all)* and time *(not yet, later, now, soon, before, after, will, already)* ___ May use irregular past tense verb forms correctly at first (such as *ran, went, made*) only to change them later and apply the past tense rule *(runned, goed, maked)* ___ Uses past tense verb form *-ed* such as *walked, played, baked* ___ Uses articles *a/an, the* ___ Uses reflexive pronouns: *myself, yourself, himself, herself, ourselves, themselves*

	SPEECH DEVELOPMENT	LANGUAGE DEVELOPMENT
PRESCHOOL YEARS: COMPLEX COMMUNICATION *(between 3 and 5 years of hearing)*	___ May mispronounce or omit some speech sounds: *l, r, v, th,* and consonant blends (*br, st, pl, skr,* etc.) Usually hearing children pronounce all of the sounds correctly in words by 7 years of age.	___ Uses complete, well-formed sentences most of the time, with increasingly complex grammar ___ Sentences are usually more than 4 words long: *"I want to play soccer."* *" I am so hungry!"* *"Where is Grandma going?"* ___ Practices language while playing, such as pretending toys are talking to each other ___ Enjoys listening to stories read aloud and attempts to read familiar books by memory ___ Uses verb forms *is/are, do/ does, have/has, can, will, had* in statements and questions, such as *"He has to eat his carrots before having ice cream,"* and *"Do I need to have a bath?"* ___ Uses negatives: *no, not, don't;* then *isn't, aren't, can't, couldn't, won't, wouldn't, doesn't*

For a suggested list of words, spoken and signed, that you can model, see Chapter 24: Ideas for Home, Play and Away.

WHAT ARE THE DO'S AND DON'TS OF MODELLING

I can —

- Respond positively to my child's communication attempts — errors and all.

- Reinforce my child's communication attempts (*"I hear you. You want the cow."*) and provide the **correct version** of what he wants to say.

- Avoid negative words and directions like this: *"No, wrong. Say ...."*

- Model the correct sound, word, or sentence to affirm my child's attempt, instead of telling my child that he has made a mistake. In this way, he feels successful and is motivated to match what I do and say.

I can respond positively and model what my baby is trying to communicate.

MODELLING CORRECT SPEECH AND WORDS (SIGNED OR SPOKEN)

When your child *incorrectly* uses speech *sounds*, you can demonstrate the *correct sound.*

CHILD'S COMMUNICATION ATTEMPT	ADULT'S POSITIVE RESPONSE
She says, reaching up, *"Uh uh."*	You say, *"Up, up."*
She says, at snack time, *"Booo."*	You say, *"Juuuice. Want juice."*
He says, observing the neighbour's pet, *"Bi dod."*	You say, *"Big dog. You're right."*
He says, *"Wuh."*	You say, *"Water. Mmmm (nodding). Water."*
He says, *"Tat ood."*	You say, *"Cat wants fffood"*

When your child uses *inappropriate* spoken *words*, you can use the *appropriate words.*

CHILD'S COMMUNICATION ATTEMPT	ADULT'S POSITIVE RESPONSE
He says, *"Cat,"* pointing to picture of a lion.	You say, *"Big cat. It's called lion."*
He says, *"Where you went?"*	You say, *"Where did I go? I went...."*
She says, *"Me big!"*	You say, *"I am big — yes, you are big!"* or *"I am big, too!"* or *"I am small!"* (Hold a doll or make yourself smaller.)
He says, *"We not eating."*	You say, *"We are not eating now."* or *"We are eating later. Yes, we will eat later."*

*When your child **signs** a word **incorrectly**, you can demonstrate the **correct sign***

CHILD'S COMMUNICATION ATTEMPT	ADULT'S POSITIVE RESPONSE
He claps fists together when you stop playing peek-a-boo, indicating *"more."*	You sign, *"more,"* showing fingertips touching — the right way.
She signs, *"Daddy home,"* with **home** hand going from one cheek to another instead of mouth to cheek.	You sign, *"home, Daddy home"* and emphasize **home** by purposefully putting your hand to your mouth, then to your cheek.
He signs, *"No airplane. All gone,"* when he can't find his toy. His sign for *airplane* has the thumb and pinky out but not the index finger (looks like the letter y, which is easier to form).	You sign, *"Airplane gone?"* and help your child to extend his index finger if he lets you. Or continue looking for the airplane while you show the sign.
He signs, *"Car"* and picks up a truck.	You pick up a car and sign, *"Yes, car."* Then pick up the truck and sign *"Truck, truck."*

*When your child uses **inappropriate signed vocabulary**, you can demonstrate the **appropriate sign***

CHILD'S COMMUNICATION ATTEMPT	ADULT'S POSITIVE RESPONSE
He signs, *"That tree big,"* pointing to a tall, thin tree.	You sign, *"Yes, tall (or high). That tree (is) tall."*

WHY IS MY CHILD MAKING MISTAKES?

If you're concerned about your child using incorrect sounds or words (spoken or signed), or not using certain sounds or words, it's important to consider some of the reasons why.

My child --

- May not hear some — or any — speech sounds.

  Parent: *"Jim is not yet using hearing aids full-time, and we model correct signs, along with the spoken word."*

- Just barely detects most speech sounds with his hearing aids on.

  Parent: *"We have to make sure that when we are modelling language with Elaine there isn't any background noise, and we are right beside her."*

- Hears all the speech sounds with his hearing aids on but often confuses words and sounds.

  Parent: *"Since Barb has a hard time telling the difference between some sounds, I try to use more words with those sounds. I emphasize the difference between the sounds without making her feel she's wrong."*

- Misses many words when I'm talking to him from more than three-feet away.

  Parent: *"I'm always reminding Ben's sister not to talk to him just as she's leaving the room, because Ben can't detect the sounds at a distance. She's a teenager and finds it hard to just sit still."*

- May have other challenges which make learning to speak or sign more difficult.

  Parent: *"We've been modelling the same things over and over for four months now. It's hard not to get frustrated."*

- Isn't using certain sounds and words (spoken or signed) perfectly, but hearing children the same age aren't using them perfectly either.

  Grandparent: *"It's easy to get focused on all the mistakes my grandson makes, but I have to remember that his parents made the same mistakes when they were his age."*

PART III: MOVING FORWARD IN CONVERSATIONS

Congratulations!

You've learned how to begin communicating with your deaf or hard of hearing child and how to become partners.

Now, you're ready to move forward in the rich and rewarding area of true conversations with your child. You've developed many skills from the previous chapters in this book to bring to these conversations.

Everything you know about communicating and being partners with your child — and the many ideas you've found that have worked for you in the past — will be especially helpful.

Chapter 20: Expanding My Child's Language …237

Chapter 21: Using Prompting …245

Chapter 22: Helping to Repair Conversation Breakdowns …253

Chapter 23: Advocating …269

EXPANDING MY CHILD'S LANGUAGE

How to Expand 237

By using language one step ahead of my child, I help his language grow.

HOW TO EXPAND

When you expand your child's language, your words or signs should be just one step ahead of your child **but within his reach.** This means adding between one to three more words or signs. Your sentences should be typical of the type of language your child is **almost** ready to use. When you're only one step ahead of your child, he is more likely to attempt to copy you. If your own sentences are long and complex, he'll probably lose interest in the conversation.

Listen and watch your child's gestures, sounds, words, or signs. Attempt to understand the **whole** message that your child is trying to tell you.

Then, repeat your child's gestures, sounds, words or signs and add a few more of your own. This lets your child know that you understand him. It gives him the opportunity to hear or see the model of a more complete sentence and to learn new words. The principles of expanding your child's language remain the same whether you are using English or American Sign Language. The conversations in this chapter are examples of parents using English.

When you add words to your child's message, try to vary the kinds of words you add.

When parents are first learning sign language and have only a few words they can sign, trying to expand their child's language can seem difficult. Often, parents find themselves using the same words repeatedly, because they know the signs for these words.

Hint: Before you engage in a play session or an activity with your child, try to anticipate some of the words that you might need. Look these up in your signing dictionary and practice them. Then, you'll be ready to use a greater variety of signs to expand your child's language. If you're taking a sign language course, let your instructor know the kinds of home routines and play activities you do with your child. Ask your instructor to demonstrate the signs you want to be able to use.

In the following example, the parent is only expanding with words that describe colour.

CHILD	MOTHER
"Ball"	"**Green** ball"
"Amandeep's ball"	Amandeep's **blue** ball"
"Big doggie"	"Yes, big **black** doggie"

Here are some additional ways this parent might have expanded the child's message —

CHILD	MOTHER
"Ball"	*"**Big** ball. Ball goes **fast**."*
"Amandeep's ball"	*"Amandeep's ball **is stuck**. Ball **under the chair**. Amandeep's ball is **dirty**. **You want** Amandeep's ball."*
"Big doggie"	*"Big doggie **scared you**. Big doggie **is eating**. **You like** the big doggie. The big doggie is **soft**."*

Remember —

- Repeat your child's gestures, sounds, words or signs.
- Add a few of your own.

Possibilities for expanding your child's language are limitless. Every situation offers opportunities as here —

CHILD	GRANDFATHER
"Fish"	*"Fish swimming. Fish swimming **fast**."*
"Swimming"	*"Yes, fish swimming. Two fish swimming."*
"Uh, oh. All gone"	*"The fish are all gone. They swam away. Bye bye fish."*

In the example that follows, the child is already starting to talk in short sentences (three words). The parent expands her child's language by modelling new words (tugboat, ship) or concepts and by using sentences that are just a little longer (five words) and more complex.

CHILD	MOTHER
"Look, Mommy, boat."	*"That's a tugoat. See, it's pulling the ship."*

The older girl in the next illustration is helping her little sister learn new words by —

- Following her sister's lead in the conversation and talking about the same topic: the birds eating.

- Expanding her sister's language through modelling sentences that are just a step ahead.

- Making her own sentences a little longer, adding a bit more information, and introducing a few new words (seagulls, fighting).

CHILD	SISTER
"Birds! Birds eating."	*"The birds are eating bread. Look, two birds are fighting. They want the bread."*
"Birds eating bread."	*"Yes, lots of birds eating bread. Those birds are called seagulls."*

In the next example, Brayden's language is a little more developed than that of the children in the previous illustrations. His mother is modelling sentences which use English grammatical structures that are more advanced, such as "is going" and "will fix."

CHILD	MOTHER
"Going on a train."	*"The man is going on the train. He's going for a ride."*
"Brayden fix it, train."	*"You will fix the train."*

CHAPTER 21

USING PROMPTING

A Note About Conversations With Deaf and
Hard of Hearing Children 245
What Is Prompting? 246
When Do I Use Prompting? 247
Prompting Throughout the Day 248

A NOTE ABOUT CONVERSATIONS WITH DEAF AND HARD OF HEARING CHILDREN

Moving forward in conversation is a difficult task for young language-learning children. They need the loving support and encouragement of the adults around them to teach them when and how to participate in conversations.

Children learn a great deal about conversation by what they overhear from others having conversation around them. In this respect young deaf and hard of hearing children are at a disadvantage: conversations that others might overhear are often out of their range of sight or hearing.

Since most people do not know or use signs, those children who use sign language as their main way of communicating seldom have a chance to "overhear" signed conversation around them.

For these reasons, adults who remember to model good conversations for their children are helping them learn to be good conversationalists. For families who are choosing to use sign language with their children, it's important to **sign all conversations** — even ones that the child might not be involved in. This strategy lets the child "overhear" a conversation in the same way hearing children do.

Parents who learn to encourage their children to participate in conversations are rewarded by ever-increasing dialogue with them.

WHAT IS PROMPTING?

Prompting is an effective way to help keep conversations going with your young deaf or hard of hearing child.

Prompts can be **nonverbal** (actions, gestures or sounds) or **verbal** (spoken words or signs).

Prompts can be either **subtle** or **more obvious.**

Here are some ways to prompt your child to stay in conversations with you —

- Look expectantly at your child by opening your eyes wider, raising your eyebrows, or tilting your head.

- Touch your child gently.

- Smile at your child.

- Say/sign, *"Your turn."*

- Say/sign, *"You know (what to say or do)."* Or, *"You need to tell me what you want."*

- Use open-ended questions which have no right or wrong answer but encourage children to come up with an idea. For instance, *"I wonder . . . ." "What might happen if . . . ." "What do you think?" "What can we do about this?"*

Remember: Prompting requires **waiting time.** When you prompt, **wait** for your child to pick up on your prompt. If you're worried that you'll lose your child's attention, prompt him one more time. Then model the words or signs you were encouraging your child to use.

From a parent:

"I learned to encourage Danny in more subtle ways, like nodding or looking expectantly, instead of always telling him, 'You talk. Tell Daddy. Say this. Say that.' Nag, nag, nag. We both found subtle prompting more effective."

I can prompt my child by looking expectantly, smiling, or touching.

WHEN DO I USE PROMPTING?

Prompting can be used naturally in any conversation to encourage your child to participate. It is appropriate to use prompting when —

- Your child does not seem to know taking a turn is expected.

- He seems reluctant to take a turn in the conversation.

You can use **prompting** when you're sure that your child has the skills to participate in a conversation. If your child doesn't yet have the necessary speech or language to follow prompting, he's not ready for you to use this more advanced conversation tool. Spend more time demonstrating turn-taking.

A word of caution: Be careful about overusing prompting to engage your child in conversation. Prompting is most effective when used to keep the conversation going. If prompting is overused, it becomes more of a command — **not** helpful in encouraging better conversation.

I can help my child know what to say next by prompting.

PROMPTING THROUGHOUT THE DAY

You can use prompting during home routines and play. Use these ideas to get you started. Then think of others that will work for you.

Getting Dressed: If your child enjoys music, try singing (*"This is the way we put on our ..."* to the tune of *"Here we go round the mulberry bush"*) as you put on each item of clothing. When you get to the name of the item, pause, hold up the clothing, and wait for your child to say the name. Then put that piece of clothing on. As your child's ability increases, leave more and more words off for him to fill in.

Setting the Table: As you set the table, name each dish, fork, spoon, cup and so on. Also, who it's for. To prompt your child to add to the conversation, hold up an item, start to name it, but then don't finish. Look expectantly at your child to complete the sentence. When he fills in the word, hand him the item to put on the table.

Say: *"Here's a plate for Mom, a plate for Jamie, and a plate for ..."* Help your child contribute to the conversation by saying, *"Mom always has a cup, but Jamie has a glass. Dad and Gayle need something to drink from, too."*

Laundry: Before you start the laundry, you can involve your child in the task by getting the laundry basket or clothes hamper and saying, *"We have a job to do. I need help."* Encourage your child to gather up her own dirty clothes and to say, *"I can help."* Once you have your child's cooperation, sort the clothes together and start a conversation about the clothes or the task. To prompt your child to add to the conversation, hold up the clothes, smile and wait. Your child can then add the name of the clothing, the person it belongs to, or something else about it — the colour, the fact it's a favourite item, it's too small, it's for school or play and so on.

Community Outings: Before you go shopping, show your child a picture of the store (simple sketches are perfect), or a book about shopping. Get out paper and pencil and encourage your child to help you write the shopping list. For example, if you're going to the grocery store, show an empty milk carton and say, *"We need more milk."* As you talk about each item, write it down on your list. To prompt your child to contribute, you can say, *"What else do we need?"* Then write the suggestions down. (Store coupons and flyers that have pictures of food items are also helpful.)

Indoor Play: Let your child be the one who leads. If you know your child can contribute more to the conversation than he's doing, decrease the amount of talking you are doing to prompt him to say more. You can also be a bit "tricky." Pretend not to understand how to play. This may prompt your child to take more of a leading role — to tell you what is happening in the play and what you should do. Be cautious with this so that your child doesn't feel that what he's doing is wrong or that he should follow your lead. To help your child add to the conversation, use comments. Then pause and wait for him to fill in the missing words: *"Your tower is very tall. Here is another blue block. Here is . . . ."*

When you and your child are playing with dolls or puppets, use props to set the scene (pretend food, a baby bottle, dress-up clothes, and so on). Take on the role of one of the dolls or puppets, and use actions or words that can help your child to go on with the conversation in the play. Pretend to be the baby doll and start to *"cry."* When your child pretends he's taking care of you, add more ideas: *"My tummy hurts. I'm hungry. I lost my bottle."* This gives your child more things to talk about.

Outdoor Play: On the swings, get your child poised and ready for a big push. Then stop while she is suspended in space above you. Smile encouragingly and wait for your child to say *"push"* or *"swing"* or *"Mommy, give me a big push."*

Reading A Book: Position yourself so your child can see the book and your face and hands at the same time. To direct your child's attention to the parts of the story you're reading or talking about, point to the pictures. To prompt your child to add to the story, have an expectant look

From a parent:

"Debbie and I loved singing simple nursery rhymes (such as Humpty-Dumpty) together, especially if we could make up actions to go with them. I'd sing a new one over and over again, especially at diaper-changing times. Then I would start to leave off the last word of the last line and wait for Debbie to fill in the word. She'd heard the rhyme so many times it was easy for her to fill in that one word. Then I'd leave the word off the end of the other lines. When Debbie could fill in all those words, I left more and more words out until she could say a whole line herself. Those little phrases came in handy throughout the day. One day when she fell off the bed she said, 'Had a great fall.'"

— and wait. Start to say a word or phrase, but wait for your child to fill in the parts. Ask open-ended questions: *"What will happen next? How does the boy feel? What do you think he should do?"*

CHAPTER 22

HELPING TO REPAIR CONVERSATION BREAKDOWNS

What Is a Conversation Breakdown? 253
Why Is Repairing a Conversation Breakdown
 Important? 255
What Causes Conversation Breakdowns? 257
Making Minor Repairs 259
Making Major Repairs 261
A Special Note on Smiling and Nodding 263
Ideas for Repairing Conversations During Home Routines
 and at Play 265

WHAT IS A CONVERSATION BREAKDOWN?

A conversation involves taking turns — talking and listening to at least one other person about the same topic. When young children are learning language, they take their turn with actions and gestures and by watching, listening and imitating. As they become more skilled in using words and/or signs to communicate their thoughts, needs and feelings, true conversations take place.

A young child's speech or signs can often be difficult to understand, especially for someone who is not familiar with the child. It's also common for young children to misunderstand what is said or signed to them. When either partner is unable to understand the other, we have a **conversation breakdown.** These breakdowns occur in conversations between hearing partners, hard of hearing partners, deaf partners, and any combination of these.

Some Examples of Conversation Breakdowns

Watch your partner for clues that a conversation may be breaking down. For example, when a partner —

- Looks confused, inattentive or disinterested.

- Seems frustrated.

- Gives inappropriate responses.

- Smiles and nods over and over again.

- Shrugs his shoulders or says *"Huh?"* or *"What?"*

WHY IS REPAIRING A CONVERSATION BREAKDOWN IMPORTANT?

When a conversation breaks down, the partners are experiencing more than the mechanics of misunderstood words or signs. Breakdowns can cause uncomfortable feelings that damage not only the conversation but self-esteem as well.

When adults take the time to repair a conversation with a child, they can keep communication going far longer. Beyond this, they're also demonstrating ways for a child to repair conversations with other partners. Although it's no one's fault if a conversation breaks down, it is the responsibility of both partners to try to repair it.

When you work to keep communication going, you're telling your child —

- You are important.

- What you have to tell me is important to me.

- Understanding me is important to you.

- I am willing to work at this with you.

- I know we can understand each other if we try.

- I love you and I care about you!

When conversations break down and no effort is made to repair the breakdown, conversation partners often give themselves negative messages. You and your child may say to yourselves —

Child: *I **know** she doesn't understand me. I don't understand her. I **feel** frustrated, angry, embarrassed, disappointed, lonely, unloved, unimportant, incompetent, afraid.*

Mother: *I **think** he isn't trying.*

Child: *I'm stupid. She doesn't care. I don't care! Why bother trying to talk/sign!*

If you play this negative self-talk record enough, you begin to believe what you say is true.

Remember: Negative self-talk is destructive. It creates a vicious circle — the more often the conversation breaks down, the more corrosive is the damage.

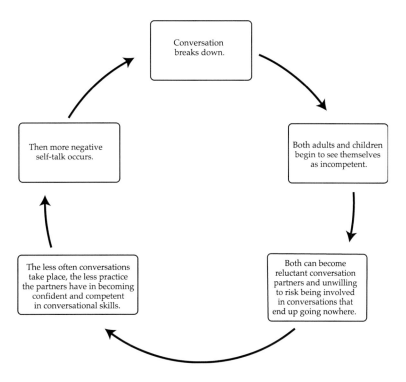

WHAT CAUSES CONVERSATION BREAKDOWNS?

There are basically four things that can go wrong in a conversation, and they can happen to either conversation partner:

1. **I can't hear/see you.** You do not clearly hear or see what the speaker is saying/signing.

   For example:

   • Background noise from a TV, a fan, running water, a noisy, crowded restaurant, or from the echo in a large gym can make it difficult to hear a conversation partner.

- Visual barriers such as poor lighting, holding a book in front of your face as you talk, signing under a table, or talking with your back to your partner can make it difficult for him to read your speech or your signs.

2. **I can't understand what you're trying to say.** You do not understand the speaker because of the way in which the message is being said or signed.

For example:

- **Words or sounds are being left out.** Your child says *"bu"* and you are not sure if he means *"ball," "bottle," "up"* or something else.

- **The speech or signing is not clear.** Your child looks as if he is signing *"dad"* but is frustrated, because what he's trying to say is *"mom."* He's just making the sign in the wrong place.

- **There is too much information or not enough.** You say to your young language-learning child, *"Let's get going; because if we don't hurry, I'll be late for work."* That's probably too many words all at once for him to understand but if you just say "work," you're not giving her enough information to get your meaning.

- **The words are all mixed up.** Your child says/ signs, *"Big dog no jump."* You may not know if he means — *"The big dog can't jump." "Don't jump, big dog." "Don't jump by the big dog."* Or, *"I can't jump over the big dog."*

I try to make sure I stay close to my baby so she can see and hear me better.

3. **I don't know what the words mean.** A young child who uses sign language may not realize that a communication partner knows only a few signs. Or an adult who is not used to talking to young children may use too many *"big"* words.

4. *I don't know what to say next.* You can hear and see what your partner is saying/signing. You're familiar with all the words and can understand your partner, but you just don't know the answer to a question or what else to say or do. (Sometimes a partner is just not interested in continuing the conversation.)

The main difference between major and minor conversation breakdowns is the amount of frustration each partner feels. What may seem like a little problem to one person can be the reason for a major explosion with another. Reading your deaf or hard of hearing child's frustration level is the key.

If you view every conversation as a time to practice the art of understanding each other's communication, then minor repairs should do the job much of the time.

On the following pages are some strategies ("repair tools") for you to try.

MAKING MINOR REPAIRS

Often, when a conversation breaks down, a few minor repairs can get it moving again.

For this to happen, it's important to —

- **Be sure I have my partner's attention before trying to communicate** (See Chapter 11 for checklist on Getting and Keeping My Child's Attention.)

- **Position myself so that my child and I can see each other clearly.** I can watch my child's body language, facial expressions and gestures for clues about what he might be saying. (See Chapter 9 for more information.)

- **Be sure my child can hear me as well as possible.** This means my child's hearing aids are on and working, and I'm using clear and appropriately loud speech. (See Chapters 2 and 6 for more information.)

- **Encourage my child to continue his turn.** I can try smiling and nodding, or looking slightly unsure or expectant. I can also give more specific encouragement by saying something like this: *"Then what happened?"* (Sometimes when your child keeps talking, he offers additional clues that may help you figure out what he's saying.)

- **Wait!** This will give both me and my child time to think about what was just said and to comprehend the words or signs.

- **Repeat what I've just said** or what I think my child has said.

- **Ask my child to repeat,** to tell me more, or tell me in a different way.

- **Rephrase:** Try to use other words, phrases or signs that my child knows.

- **Add words, signs, actions or gestures** to clarify what I'm saying. For example, if my child doesn't understand when I say, *"There's a dog,"* I can try pointing at the dog or saying/signing, *"There's a big, brown dog."*

From a parent:

"The hardest part about communicating with Greg is when we don't understand each other. It's so frustrating. Sometimes it moves me to tears. But I'm determined to have the best communication I can with my son, and I will never stop trying to understand him and helping him to understand me. I'm rewarded every day by his patience and his love."

From a parent:

"Whenever Jenny didn't understand us, we'd repeat what we had said. But if that didn't help, we were really stuck about what else to do. What helped us was to use other approaches — adding a few words, acting things out, or using different words. She's learned to try different ways of helping us understand her, too."

- **Say the key word.** This helps my child understand what I'm talking about (the topic) so that the other words make more sense.

- **Give feedback** to make it easier for my child to know whether or not he understands me and how **much** he understands. For example: If I say, *"The baby is crying,"* and my child seems to understand, I can verify this by adding, *"Yes, the baby is crying."* But if he seems to be confusing the words, I might say, *"Not the **lady**, the **baby**."*

- **Follow my child's lead** if I'm not sure what to say next. I can imitate his actions or words. I can talk about what he is doing or what he might be feeling or thinking. The goal is to keep the communication going as long as possible.

Remember: When you repair a conversation, you're showing your child how to do the same thing. Use the words you want your child to use. Some examples: *"Say it again." "It's too loud." "Speak slowly." "I don't understand. Show me." "I can't hear you. The TV's too loud." "Tell me more." "Did you say . . . ?"*

MAKING MAJOR REPAIRS

Sometimes a conversation really heads for the rocks with puzzled or angry partners glaring at each other (or even worse — turning away from each other). What can be done to save the conversation and each partner's self-esteem?

I can —

- **Be flexible with my language level.** If my level is not appropriate for my child, I'll likely find conversation breakdowns are happening frequently.

(Don't be afraid to go back and simplify your language when either you or your child become frustrated in a conversation.)

I can learn to use many tools for major repairs.

- **Be creative.** I can try getting my message across in a different way.

  For example I might —

  Draw a picture (always keep a pencil and paper handy).

  Find a related picture in a book or magazine.

  Use gestures, actions or mime to act out my meaning. (See Chapter 9 for more information about nonverbal communication.)

- **Apologize.** Let my child know how sorry I am that right now I'm having trouble understanding or being understood, but that this temporary setback in no way means I love him less. (Smiles and hugs can be very reassuring when tensions are high.)

From a parent:

"I've learned always to check to be sure Michael understands what I've said. But I know other people think he understands them when he doesn't. That's because he's great at smiling and nodding and saying 'yes' when they ask him, 'Did you understand me?' Or, 'Do you mean this?' It makes everything seem OK for the moment, but it doesn't really help him to learn in the long run. I really appreciate it when others take the time to be sure Michael is actually following the conversation."

- **Take a break.** Tell my child, *"Let me think about that."* Maybe my child is (or I am) feeling too tired or sick or rushed to give much energy to the conversation. (Sometimes, when the stress of the moment is gone, you have the freedom to think about the conversation and what went wrong. You can also wait awhile and then return to the conversation with a new attitude.)

- **Ask for help.** Frequently, someone else can help me get my idea across, or interpret what my child is saying or signing. (Caution: Don't rely on another person to "rescue" you every time a conversation starts to falter.) While getting a third person involved in the conversation can be helpful at times, working on the repairs yourself gives you many more skills in creating better conversations with your deaf or hard of hearing child.

Remember: When you take time to repair a conversation with your child, you're not only teaching him how to do this, but you're also showing him how much you love him and how important it is to you that you communicate — even when the going gets rough.

If you or your child are constantly frustrated by conversation breakdowns when you use speech alone, you may want to consider adding signs to your spoken language. See Chapter 14 for more information.

A SPECIAL NOTE ON SMILING AND NODDING

Smiling and Nodding to your conversation partner can say, *"Keep going. I'm interested in you and what you're saying, and I understand."* (This is a help to your partner.)

Smiling and Nodding can also mean, *"I did not understand you, but keep going. I'm interested in you. Maybe if you keep going, I'll eventually understand what you're saying."* (This is also a help.)

Smiling and Nodding, however, can have a different meaning: *"I did not understand you, but if I smile and nod you'll think I understand, and I won't get 'caught' and then feel stupid."* (This is **not** recommended.)

Good conversation partners use — but do not overuse — smiling and nodding to keep conversations going. They smile and nod to encourage and maintain a conversation, but they are willing to risk feeling uncomfortable by admitting it when there is a conversation breakdown that needs a repair.

Good conversation partners make sure the other person understands. They can check by asking, *"What did I say?"* Or by asking relevant comprehension questions: *"Who?"* … *"What?"* … *"Where?"*… *"When?"*… *"Why?"*

Asking, *"Do you understand?"* encourages more smiling and nodding and is not as helpful.

Remember: What you do in a conversation is a model for your child to follow. If you use smiling and nodding when you fail to understand your child's communication, your child will begin to use smiling and nodding in that way, too. Better to use a repair strategy than to allow conversation to continue when you have no idea what your partner is saying.

IDEAS FOR REPAIRING CONVERSATIONS DURING HOME ROUTINES AND AT PLAY

You and your child may find times each day when your conversations need a repair. Here are some examples of conversation breakdowns and possible "repair tools" to use. Try some out for yourself, and see which ones work for you. Then add your own ideas, too.

Eating: If your child wants something and has limited language, you can tell him *"show me."* Point to a number of different food choices until he nods *"yes"*. Then use

Banana! You want the banana.

the correct word or sign. If this happens fairly frequently at mealtime, you might make up a set of food cards to correspond to the foods you serve often. Your child can find the picture card for the food he wants. You can then show him the correct speech or sign for that food.

Housekeeping: If your child frequently tries to communicate when there is a lot of background noise from the vacuum, dishwasher, clothes dryer and so on, you can show him what to do. Say/sign *"It's too noisy. I can't hear you. Wait."* Remove the background noise and tell him, *"That's better. Now I can hear you. What do you want to tell me?"*

Bathtime: Because hearing aids are not worn during bathtime, there is a greater chance for miscommunication to occur, especially for those children who find their hearing aids essential in conversations. This is a good time to practice speech reading and/or sign language with your child. Tell him *"You can't hear me. No hearing aids. Watch!"*

Community Outings: Many times strangers will smile or talk with your young child when you're out shopping. These little chats can be difficult for you and for your child. This is a good opportunity for you to help others understand hearing loss. Say, *"My child has a hearing loss. He can understand you better if you look directly at him, speak clearly, and use gestures."* As your child achieves increasing success communicating with unfamiliar people, he's building his self-esteem.

Bedtime: One of the best ways to end a day is with a time of shared quiet conversation or play. Be sure your child can see you by keeping a light on — and hear you by keeping hearing aids on — until the final *"Goodnight."* Some children prefer a night light all night so that they can feel in touch with their environment when their hearing aids are off.

Indoor Play: When you play with blocks, trucks or other toys on the floor, and your child takes a turn in the conversation (but you're unsure what he has said), use the toys to act out different ideas. Ask *"Like this?"* Or, *"Is this right?"* Or *"I think you said . . . ."* Then watch for a response. This keeps the focus on the play and helps conversation continue for a few more turns.

Pretending to be different characters — for example, a parent or teacher or doctor — offers many opportunities for your child to be "in charge" of a conversation. For instance, he can practice telling you: "Watch. Pay attention. Turn the light on so you can see me." It also gives you a chance to be a little mischievous in your role as child, student, or patient and for your child to see another view of himself.

Puppets or dolls are another way to play out different roles and are especially fun for children or adults who are shy about acting out a role themselves.

For older children, pictures of problem situations (for example, a TV on in the background while a parent is trying to talk to the child) are good ways to start discussions and help lead to solutions.

Outdoor Play: When children are outside, they're often too far out of range for hearing aids and speech reading to be of much help. Tell your child *"You're too far away to hear me."* Try using signs and gestures to put your message across. Encourage your child to get into the habit of staying within your view — for conversation as well as safety.

Reading books: Books offer a positive way to keep a conversation going. If you or your child are still unsure about what the other has said/signed after several repeats or rephrases, you can always turn the page and try again.

CHAPTER 23

ADVOCATING

Becoming an Effective Advocate for Your Child 269
Self-Advocacy: How to Help Your Child Become an Effective
    Self-Advocate 286

BECOMING AN EFFECTIVE ADVOCATE FOR YOUR CHILD

What Is Advocacy?

From a parent:

"I don't want to be looked down on by professionals. Remember, they are the experts in their field; but I am the expert on my child. So, if we come together and listen to each other, it will work beautifully.

From a parent:

"We see our children 24 hours a day. Professionals may only see our children two hours a week, or even once a month. So parents have a strong idea of what their child's needs are, and professionals should listen to us."

Advocacy is the act of pleading or arguing in favour of something. When parents are being an advocate for their child, they are speaking out or intervening with others on behalf of their child.

Why Do You Need to Learn How to Advocate for Your Child?

Who can be the best advocate for your child? You! You have your child's best interests at heart. Therapists, doctors, audiologists, and other professionals will probably only know your child for a few years. You will know your child for a life-time. You know your child better than anyone else, and so you should play an active role in making decisions about your child's education and therapy.

As parents we know our own children. We are usually aware of their personality, their likes and dislikes, their needs and strengths. Sometimes we need to give constructive criticism to the people working with our children (teachers, audiologists, doctors, communication specialists, etc.). Other times we need to speak out on behalf of our children in order to get services for them. You can't assume you or your child will get what is needed **automatically**. Often you will get something if you ask for it. When resources are limited, "the squeaky wheel gets the grease" — at least to a certain extent. However, there are good and poor ways to "squeak."

Good therapy or educational services are intensive and expensive. Resources are limited. If you have a child with a hearing loss, you may sometimes find yourself fighting for services for your child. To succeed, you will need information, skills, and tools.

Children who are deaf or hard of hearing have a basic right to access. When parents are actively involved in advocating for their children, they are less likely to be forgotten and more likely to get the best, most appropriate service.

How to Begin to Advocate For Your Child

Gather Information

Your first step in becoming an advocate is to gather information. You need to become an expert on your child's hearing loss and communication and learning needs. Then you can more clearly identify what your child needs and what services or supports you should request. In addition, you may find yourself in the position of educating others about your child.

Read everything you can get your hands on. Talk with other parents. Contact your National and Provincial or State organizations that offer help and information for parents of children with a hearing loss. On-line support groups are easily found on the Web. Research these groups carefully until you find one with members who seem to be knowledgeable.

As you become better informed, you will find it easier to evaluate services being provided to your child. It will

From a parent:

"Professionals don't know everything! Trust your gut. It's okay to question what professionals tell you. It's your right to get second opinions."

From a parent:

"I never thought I could become a good advocate for my child. Professionals have many other kids to deal with. Parents have to convey the information about their child's needs to everyone. If you don't do it, no one else will!"

From a parent:

"In the beginning I had no confidence as a parent. I have learned to share my thoughts and ideas with others, and I have become more assertive. I amaze myself sometimes!"

From a parent:

"Become really informed about all the issues related to your child's hearing loss. It is hard to do this, because at first you feel so overwhelmed. But you need to do a lot of research in order to make good decisions for your child."

From a parent:

"At first it can be difficult to speak up on behalf of your child, especially if you tend to be shy. It is not always easy to question doctors or teachers. Take little steps in the beginning, and you will learn how to become a strong advocate."

From a parent:

"Professionals are people, too, and they are frequently very busy. I have learned that it is important to make sure I also give positive feedback to professionals. I always thank them for their time and effort. I let them know when their information or support has been helpful, and I write thank-you notes whenever I think the professional has gone beyond the call of duty. I believe my recognition of their efforts helps to encourage and motivate them to continue doing their very best for my child."

also help you to better understand what professionals are telling you about your child.

You should take time to learn more about your child's legal rights to services. Find out about the organizations and schools providing services in your community.

Become Informed: Sources of Information

Today, through the use of the Internet, parents have easier access to information than parents in previous generations. If you do not have a computer or are not hooked up to the Internet, you may be able to use the Internet at your local library. Tell the librarian the type of information you are looking for, and she can help you learn how to search helpful Websites. (See Appendix A for a listing of helpful Websites as well as informational books and videos/DVDs).

Learn to be Assertive

Parents should not assume that the professionals working with their child are "mind-readers" and know how the parent feels about what is happening to their child. It helps to communicate clearly and directly. Some parents worry that if they assert themselves, the professionals working with their child may view the parents as being "aggressive;" and this negative impression may impact the service to their child. But there are significant differences between being aggressive, assertive, and passive. To become an effective advocate for your child you will want to learn to become **assertive**.

Styles of communicating — What you may experience

Assertive: Parents state their opinions, feelings, and their child's needs clearly and firmly while continuing to be respectful of others. Parents who use an assertive style often feel more self-confident in their interactions with the professionals working with their child. Professionals usually appreciate knowing where the parent stands, and they typically respond more positively. This is true even when they are unable to immediately give the parent what they want. **Being assertive will help you to advocate more effectively for your child.**

Aggressive: Parents express their opinions in a hostile or confrontational manner and do not listen to the opinions of others. These parents will often interrupt or try to talk over others. They may also verbally attack those they do not agree with. Parents who use an aggressive style of communicating may discover that professionals often become more defensive or angry when they are verbally attacked. So they are then less able to calmly listen and respond to the parent's concerns. **Being aggressive will**

usually NOT help you to be an effective advocate for your child.

Passive: Parents state their opinions hesitantly — or don't state their own opinions, feelings and needs at all. When the professional discounts or ignores the parent's opinion, the parent stays silent. Parents who are passive may end up feeling helpless, ignored, and angry at themselves or at the professionals. **Being passive will NOT help you to be an effective advocate for your child.**

Practice #1 — Identifying Assertive, Passive, and Aggressive Styles

When you read the definitions of assertive, aggressive and passive styles you may have decided you want to change your own style of communicating. Changing from a passive or aggressive style of communicating to an assertive style takes practice.

Read through the following statements and decide whether the parent is using an **assertive, aggressive,** or **passive** style.

Then go back to the examples that you felt were aggressive or passive. Write down some alternative statements that could be considered assertive, rather than aggressive or passive. The key is at the bottom of the list.

1. Parent says to friend:

   "I don't think that program is right for my child; he seems so unhappy there. But they are the experts, and they have lots of experience. I doubt they would even listen to my opinion."

   Style: _____

2. Parent says to teacher:

   "What do you mean my child has a learning problem? If he has trouble learning, it's because you have no experience with hard of hearing children. You haven't done a single thing to help my child."

   Style: _____

3. Parent says to audiologist:

   "I understand that my son's cochlear implant speech processor has taken longer to repair than expected. I also realize you would like for me to return the loaner. However, my son is at a critical learning age and needs consistent input. As soon as my son's processor is repaired I will immediately return the loaner."

   Style: _____

4. Parent says to teacher:

   "What do you mean you think we should talk to the counsellor? There's nothing wrong with our family. If he is misbehaving at preschool, it's because your class is completely out of control. How do you think my son is supposed to learn in a class like yours?"

   Style: _____

5. Parent complains to friend:

   "During story time at preschool the teachers tend to speak very quietly when they are reading, because they think this keeps the kids' attention. Of course, when that happens my daughter can't hear the story — especially when the teachers also play music in the background! I wish those teachers knew more about hearing loss, but you know . . . what can you do?"

   Style: _____

6. Parent says to family doctor:

"I understand that you don't think my child is old enough to be referred for speech therapy. However, I have been reading about the importance of early intervention, and I feel it is essential for my child's speech and language to be assessed as soon as possible. Will you be able to make a referral, or should I obtain a referral from someone else?

Style: _____

7. Parent of a two-year-old child talking to speech/ language pathologist:

"I don't believe those test results. My child had never even seen those pictures before! And I don't see how you can make judgments about my child's learning level. I mean . . . how would you know? You don't even have any children yourself!"

Style: _____

8. Parent of an 18-month-old to teacher of the deaf and hard of hearing:

"I really appreciated the time you spent developing those home ideas. I need to tell you, though, that I found some of them did not work as well as I had hoped. For instance, my daughter really does not enjoy activities like those with the animals in the barn. She really loves looking at books, though. Is there a way we could do some listening activities while we read books?"

Style: _____

9. Parent of an 8-month-old talking to audiologist:

"You explained the reasons why it takes two weeks to get earmolds back, and I understand that no other

parents have ever complained before. However, I am very concerned. My daughter is growing so quickly these days that her ear molds are not lasting very long. I don't want her to miss out on learning, because we are constantly waiting for ear molds to come back. I would like to work together with you to find some other solution to this serious problem."

Style:_____

10. Parent to friend:

"Last week when I was in the preschool, I noticed that they still are not using the FM equipment with my son. I heard one of the teachers complain she did not like wearing the headset with the microphone, because it messed up her hair! I've already had to tell the teachers that my son is allergic to peanut butter. I'm afraid to bother them again; I'd probably get a reputation for being too pushy and then they might take it out on my son — or they might decide it's just too much trouble having him in their school."

Style: _____

KEY

1. Passive	2. Aggressive	3. Assertive	4. Aggressive	5. Passive
6. Assertive	7. Aggressive	8. Assertive	9. Assertive	10. Passive

Practice # 2 — Describing Concerns in Real-Life Situations

Here are some real-life situations parents found themselves facing. Pretend you are in each situation, and consider how you could communicate your concerns in an assertive way.

Situation # 1

Your son is profoundly deaf, uses a cochlear implant, and is in kindergarten. Last spring, when you attended a meeting with the school district, they promised the following:

- Individual speech and language sessions **once a week.**

- A meeting with the classroom teacher and the teacher of the deaf and hard of hearing at the beginning of the year to help establish goals for your child in the classroom.

There is a problem. Your child is only receiving individual speech and language sessions **once a month.** You were not invited to provide input to your child's Individualized Educational Plan, and you have just received a copy of the Individualized Educational Plan from the teacher who asked you to sign it. You do not agree with some aspects of the plan.

Finding Your Voice: How Would You Express Your Concerns?

Situation # 2

You attend a parent group, and recently the sessions have not focused on topics that were of interest to you. The person who leads the group is enthusiastic about the group, so you hate to give negative feedback. You don't want to hurt her feelings. However, you are finding you have to drag yourself to these sessions. You wish the sessions could focus on topics more relevant to your life.

Finding Your Voice: How Would You Express Your Concerns?

Situation # 3

Your two-year-old child has a moderate to severe hearing loss. The speech-language pathologist working with you recently completed an assessment on your child. You do not feel this assessment reflects your child's real abilities, and you wish she had included some of your home observations in the report. In addition, you are finding that some of her ideas for speech therapy activities at home are not working very well. She is a nice person, and she really seems to care about your child. You are worried that she will feel criticized if you give her feedback. You also worry that she might feel offended, and then that will affect how she works with you and your child.

Finding Your Voice: How Would You Express Your Concerns?

When Should You Become More Assertive?

Parents of young children lead busy and often stressful lives. Sometimes parents need to decide when to put the time and effort into taking action on behalf of their child. The questions in the box below might help you decide when you need to become more assertive.

DECIDING WHEN TO BE ASSERTIVE

How do I know when action is called for?

1. Do I understand the situation clearly? Have I heard both sides?

2. How important is this to me or my child? Will assertive action achieve something important?

3. What is the likelihood there will be a positive result?

4. Am I looking for a positive outcome or do I just want to express myself?

5. What are the options?

6. Am I prepared to act in an appropriately assertive way?

7. Have I counted to ten? Have I taken time to consider the situation? Have I defused my angry feelings, and am I ready to express myself rationally?

8. Would it be better to wait until tomorrow? Will the other person be more receptive later?

9. Will I kick myself later if I do not take action now?

10. What are the possible consequences from my being assertive in this situation?

11. Will my being assertive in this situation help to make changes?

Based on *Your Perfect Right!* by R. Alberti & M. Emmons

WORKING WITH MY CHILD'S TEAM OF PROFESSIONALS

You are becoming an advocate for your child by staying informed and getting involved. What is your role when working with professionals? What are some ways that make it easier to be an advocate on your child's team?

My Role Is:

- To inform people about my child's listening and communication needs. I am an expert when it comes to knowing my own child.

Often parents communicate by talking with the professionals involved with their child. However, there are times when the most effective form of communication is a formal letter. This is particularly true when you are making a specific request, when certain issues need to be clarified, when you need to state facts in a chronological order, or when you are in disagreement with a proposed plan for your child.

- To be an active member of the team by helping to monitor my child's progress and by staying in touch with the professionals providing services.

  Keeping in touch includes: collaborating with professionals about ways to implement recommendations, having realistic expectations, and giving feedback to the professionals about recommended strategies and techniques you are practicing to help your child's communication development.

- In order to relate useful information to others, request written and videotaped information from professionals. This information could be in the form of assessment results, checklists, long and short-term goals, and recommended techniques, strategies, resources, and activities.

Parents have been able to combine what they know about their own child with professional documentation in the form of "introduction letters" for new teachers, caregivers, coaches, babysitters, and relatives. On the next page is an example of an introduction letter.

SAMPLE LETTER OF INTRODUCTION TO PROFESSIONALS

From Jesse Kazemir's parents

Jesse has a **permanent moderately-severe hearing loss** in both ears. He wears a **bone-conduction hearing aid.** With his hearing aid, he hears well in very quiet surroundings. In a group setting, where there is background noise (i.e. people talking, chairs scraping across the floor, traffic noise, motor noise from fans, radio, music, etc.), Jesse has much more difficulty hearing and understanding speech. To help Jesse understand language in the classroom it is important to ensure the following:

- Jesse should be **seated close to** and **facing the teacher** (seeing the face of the person talking helps Jesse to hear what they say, especially with background noise).

- Jesse will be most likely to understand other people in the classroom if they **take turns speaking.**

- Jesse needs to wear his hearing aid in order to hear and understand speech. An adult needs to be able to help Jesse if his hearing aid stops working (e.g. dead batteries, a problem with his wire, etc.). His hearing aid volume should be set at 3.

- Jesse needs to use an **FM system** in the classroom and during other group activities (e.g. assembly, storytime, etc.). It is very important that the FM system be working properly. If it is not working, it is **worse** than if no FM is used at all.

- Due to the nature of Jesse's hearing loss he **cannot locate sounds.** This causes him some difficulty:

    - He cannot tell which direction a vehicle noise is coming from.

    - If a person that Jesse can't see starts talking, he doesn't know where to look.

    - Jesse has a lot of trouble with hide and seek!

- If Jesse seems to be ignoring you or not listening, please give him the benefit of the doubt and check his hearing aid first.

Jesse's speech and language skills are good right now, but due to the severity and the nature of his hearing loss, he needs to be monitored by a **Speech-Language Pathologist.** Jesse will also need support from a **Teacher of the Deaf and Hard of Hearing.**

Getting Organized

Purchase a three-ring binder. Keep all of the information about your child in this binder. Organize it in a way that helps you to locate information quickly (you may need to refer to something at a meeting). You might keep the most current information at the top.

You may want to include in this binder:

- Audiology reports and audiograms.

- Reports and other documents, such as Individualized Service Plans from other professionals.

- Your own observations, notes on progress, questions, and concerns about your child.

- List of names, addresses, and phone numbers of all the professionals involved with your child.

- Log of Telephone Calls: Jot down notes about any decisions, recommendations, or disagreements.

- Notes from any meetings about your child.

TEAM MEETINGS

Sooner or later you will likely be invited to attend a team meeting about your child. This may be a meeting of professionals from a clinic, a hospital, or a school. Some parents may find these meetings intimidating. On the next page are some successful hints from other parents:

GETTING PREPARED

___ Write a list of questions and concerns you would like discussed at the meeting.

___ List your child's strengths.

___ List the things you would like your child to be able to do within the next year — your goals and objectives, the skills and knowledge you hope he will acquire. Be realistic and specific.

___ List the types of services and professionals you feel will be needed in order for those goals and objectives to be accomplished. It may be necessary for you to make some compromises. Ahead of time, consider your priorities and on which of them you are unwilling to yield.

___ List any possible disagreements or conflicts. Write down possible solutions to any of these problems. Sometimes professionals are more willing to adjust a plan or attempt to solve a problem, if you are able to suggest some possible alternatives.

___ Invite a spouse or a friend to attend with you. One of you should be prepared to take notes at the meeting. It may be possible to record the meeting on audio or videotape.

___ Bring all of your child's records and reports to the meeting.

___ Become knowledgeable about the law, your child's rights to an appropriate education, and about funding for special services. Find out what type and amount of funding your child is eligible for.

___ Request the services of a language interpreter if required. It is important to reduce the possibility of misunderstandings between you and the professionals when sharing information about your child.

AT THE MEETING

___ Be on time.

___ Find out how much time has been allowed for this meeting. State at the beginning what you want included on the agenda (what you want discussed) during this meeting.

___ Be friendly. Don't start the meeting by acting as though you are ready to do battle. (This can put professionals on the defensive, and they may be more reluctant to see things from your perspective.)

___ Take notes to help you recall specific points of discussion.

___ Ask for an explanation of any terms you do not understand. Say: "It is important to me to understand everything we discuss here today, so I may be stopping some of you to ask for clarification of a term I am not familiar with."

___ Praise team members who have been helpful, or who you feel have been doing a good job with your child.

___ Try to help solve problems (offer possible solutions), rather than lay blame.

___ Don't hesitate to question any recommendations or statements made by the professionals. Remember, the team is discussing your child!

___ If a rule or policy is mentioned, you may want to ask to see it documented in writing.

___ If you find yourself becoming too emotional, you may wish to ask for a brief break in order to collect yourself.

___ Make sure the results of the meeting are summarized at the end, and that all recommendations are clearly stated. If the professional team has agreed to provide specific services for your child, make sure you keep a record of **who** will be doing **what** and by **what date.**

___ If you are not in agreement with decisions made at this meeting, ask about the appeal process. Say: *"I am not in agreement with these decisions. I understand that I have the right to appeal this decision. I need you to inform me of the appeal process in this school district, agency (or other)."*

AFTER THE MEETING

___ Summarize your notes from the meeting. Make sure you include the specifics about any recommendations or disagreements made at the meeting. Send a copy of your notes to the other team members, including the person responsible for making funding decisions.

___ Ask for a review meeting anytime you sense problems or the need for change.

SELF ADVOCACY: HOW TO HELP YOUR CHILD BECOME AN EFFECTIVE SELF-ADVOCATE

What are Self-Advocacy Skills?

You have been advocating for your child in many different ways. You and your family meet with families who have a child with a hearing loss. You read books together about hearing loss and about children who also use a hearing device. You share information about your child's hearing and communication with others involved in her life. You are involved in your child's communication services and educational programs. To facilitate your child's communication development, you have worked to build her inner confidence, using various strategies from this book and from the recommendations of your communication specialist. You have encouraged her to communicate with others and have fostered social interactions with other children.

When your child is able to communicate — either on her own or with support — she will start to advocate for herself. If her communication interactions are successful, she is already building confidence in herself.

Self-advocacy skills begin with a certain amount of hearing-device independence — such as putting the hearing aids in a special place at night or replacing the cochlear implant coil when it falls off. A sense of ownership and pride for the hearing device at a young age is related to self-acceptance and positive feelings about oneself.

Even preschoolers can start to describe their hearing and why they use a hearing device. At the BC Family Hearing Resource Centre, preschoolers with hearing loss and their parents participate in a group program where all the children can practice hearing-device independence and maintenance. They learn about hearing and about their own unique hearing abilities and challenges, and they practice problem solving in difficult listening situations within a supportive, safe environment. It is often easier to encourage a child to advocate for himself when he has a sense of belonging — in this case, being part of a group of children who also have a hearing loss.

Other ways to achieve this sense of belonging when you may not have many similar-aged children in your community with hearing loss is through books and DVDs or videos about real deaf and hard of hearing children. You can also attend conferences related to living with hearing loss, such as the annual conferences of the Canadian Hard of Hearing Association and the Hearing Loss Association of America. You may be able to have contact by phone or email with another family that you have met through a network or an association. BC Family Hearing Resource Centre's Parent-to-Parent Support Network aims to match similar families who benefit from knowing that they have many successes and challenges in common.

Helping to Build Your Child's Self-Esteem

Research indicates that children with a hearing loss who are integrated into regular settings (such as community preschool and hearing classrooms) face unique communication challenges. While many of these children benefit academically from a mainstream education, some report feelings of isolation, loneliness, shame, inadequacy, and powerlessness. These feelings are symptomatic of low self-esteem and poor inner confidence. You can do a lot to help build your child's confidence early on by connecting some of his learning and social challenges to his hearing needs. Focusing on identifying the barriers — and overcoming these barriers — teaches your child how to have some control over difficult listening situations.

How Can I Help My Child Develop Self-Advocacy Skills?

I can —

- Make arrangements for my child to spend time with other children and adults with a hearing loss.

- Talk openly about my child's hearing loss instead of treating it as a secret — an unspoken topic.

- Help my child become comfortable with hearing aids, cochlear implants, FM equipment, or using sign language in public from an early age.

- Teach my child that he has the right to participate in conversations. Help him learn how to tell others what he needs. For example, he can say, "I can't hear you. Please turn the radio off."

- Be careful about the messages you are giving your child related to his hearing loss and listening abilities. Trying to cover the hearing aids for photographs, or telling him to do a better job of listening may give him the feeling he is not okay.

- Give your child a broad range of experiences in the community so that he has a "regular" childhood.

- Include your child in group conversations so he never feels left out.

- If signing is part of your communication, then at home everyone should sign their conversations.

- Model assertiveness by recognizing and describing your problem, concerns, or feelings out loud, asking for help, and explaining some possible solutions or actions that might solve the problem.

Helping your child feel proud and confident about who she is needs to start early — before feelings of helplessness set in. You can also give your child appropriate opportunities to advocate for herself. Self-advocacy boosts self-esteem.

CHECKLIST OF SELF-ADVOCACY SKILLS FOR YOUR CHILD

Here are some ways that your child will develop confidence related to his hearing.

My child —

___ Describes and identifies quiet sounds, loud sounds, and "just right" sounds.

___ Pushes in own earmold when there is acoustic feedback from improper insertion or loose fit.

___ Replaces the magnetic coil piece of the cochlear implant device when it falls off.

___ Replaces hearing aid casing when it comes away from behind the ear (mold still in place).

___ Increasingly becomes more independent with own hearing device: tests batteries, puts device away carefully when not in use, replaces aid or coil if accidentally removed.

___ Attempts to insert earmold(s) and turn on own hearing aids or cochlear implant.

___ Describes his own hearing loss and hearing device (name, parts, volume/ sensitivity setting, purpose of device, additional listening devices such as FM).

___ Identifies difficult listening situations, such as a noisy classroom or a gym that has echoes.

___ Demonstrates good listening habits (eliminates background noise to communicate, gets close to speaker)

___ Describes to others what makes it difficult to hear, why, and what solutions are available. These barriers to optimal listening conditions vary among individuals, but most kids agree that background noise and distance from a speaker — or not being able to see the speaker — make paying attention challenging.

___ Inserts own mold(s)

___ Identifies the fact that his hearing device isn't working well and tells an adult when there is a problem (device stopped working — or is intermittently working — or FM is not on).

PART IV: PROMOTING COMMUNICATION AND LITERACY IN ROUTINES

Whether you are just beginning to communicate with your child, or are already conversation partners, you will find the ideas in this section helpful. These are practical ways to help your child develop communication during everyday routines. The activities and suggestions can be used throughout your day, at home, play, or away.

Chapter 24: Ideas for Home, Play, and Away ...293

IDEAS FOR HOME, PLAY AND AWAY

The Importance of Linking Literacy to
Everyday Events 294

How to Use This Chapter 294

At Home
    People in Your Child's Life 295
    Describing Home 297
    Waking Up and Bedtime 298
    Changing Diapers and Toileting 300
    Bathtime 302
    Getting Dressed and Undressed 305
    Cooking 308
    Mealtime 311
    Washing Dishes 314
    Housekeeping 315
    Reading and Writing Activities 316
    Art 319

At Play
    Indoor Play 321
    Outdoor Play 324
    Entertainment 328
    Family Events and Holidays 330

Away From Home
    Shopping 333
    Community Outings and Trips 335
    Animals......336
    At the Audiologist's 337
    School......338

THE IMPORTANCE OF LINKING LITERACY TO EVERYDAY EVENTS

Reading abilities are related to communication skills. You already know from reading this book that deaf and hard of hearing children require purposeful, goal-oriented listening, speech, and language stimulation. Those communication techniques (along with professional guidance and individualized planning) are for you to use each day to promote your child's communiction development. All of the strategies in this book that build communication abilities are also helpful for reading and writing development. You can set the stage for literacy by taking these ideas one step further and associating communication with **written** information.

During daily routines, look for opportunities to connect communication with letters and their sounds. Model the importance of reading and writing for practical reasons: For instance, making grocery lists — or for enjoyment and relaxation, reading a good book before bed.

In the ideas to follow, we have included special **Literacy Bonus** suggestions to make the connection between communication, reading, and writing obvious to your child.

Practice at least one **Literacy Bonus** idea every day to build your child's love of words.

HOW TO USE THIS CHAPTER

In this final chapter, we've tried to cover the variety of experiences that make up a young child's world. Beneath each heading (for instance, Mealtime, Bathtime), you'll find suggestions that should help you to increase your child's ability with language.

The words listed for each separate activity are among the first typically learned by young children. If you're just starting sign language, you can use these word lists as a guide to help you know which signs to learn first. (Some parents request that their sign language instructor include these words in their classes.) Before a particular activity — bathtime, for instance, or a trip to the park — you can refer to the appropriate list. Then look up a few of these words in your signing dictionary so that you can use them with your child.

Vocabulary is linked to literacy; word knowledge helps build "reading readiness." By understanding the meaning of many words, you child may then begin to attach those meanings to printed words.

Along with new suggestions, you may find a few we've included from earlier chapters. Our goal in putting all of this together is to give you a quick reference that you can use during your busy, demanding days.

AT HOME

People in Your Child's Life

Words/Signs to Use: People

mommy	*boy/girl*	*aunt*
daddy	*brother*	*uncle*
baby	*sister*	*grandma*
child	*baby-sitter*	*grandpa*

- Like magnets, children are drawn to other human beings, especially to familiar family members and

Brothers and sisters can enjoy communicating with each other.

to others that they see frequently. It's important to identify the people in your child's life each time they appear.

Use photo albums to refer to the people in your child's life. Take pictures of visits to the doctor, dentist and other community people you see.

Describe the relationships between people. For example: *"Who is your cousin Kyle's mommy?"* Then add: *"Aunty Jean is my sister **and** Kyle's mommy."*

Literacy Bonus: Sound out the letters that spell family members' names. Spell their names with magnetic letters on the fridge.

Describing Home

Words/Signs to Use: Home

address	*co-op housing*	*roof*
apartment	*door*	*screen*
basement	*doorknob*	*stairs*
bathroom	*downstairs*	*sofa*
bedroom	*home*	*townhouse*
ceiling	*house*	*upstairs*
chair	*kitchen*	*wall*
closet	*living room*	*window*
condominium	*room*	

- For every young child, his own nest is the centre of his life. As you move from room to room with your child, use the words in the previous list to help him describe his home (and to increase his vocabulary).

  Involve your child in tidying up. Decide where things belong. For example: Say, *"Does your teddy bear go in the kitchen or in your bedroom?"*

  Goldilocks and the Three Bears story provides vocabulary about room and furniture in the home. Borrow picture books from the library that describe homes.

  Play hiding games and describe where in the house you, your child, or objects are hidden.

Literacy Bonus: Write your child's name on personal belongings — clothing, books, etc. Look at picture books which label dwellings and the people who live there. Take photographs of your own home for the photo album. Put your child's name on the door to his room, or near where he sleeps.

Waking Up and Bedtime

Words/Signs to Use for Waking Up in the Morning and at Bedtime

alarm	*good morning*	*sleep*
awake	*good night*	*teddy bear*
bed	*late*	*time*
blanket	*light*	*tired*
clock	*light off/on*	*today*
comb	*listen*	*tomorrow*
crib	*nap*	*toothbrush*
dark	*pillow*	*up*
early	*pyjamas*	*wake up*

In the morning, if your baby cries to let you know that he wants to be picked up, show him the next step in learning to communicate this. Greet him with a facial expression that lets him know how happy you are to see him, and lift your arms in a natural gesture that indicates wanting to be picked up. Sign/say, *"Oh, you want me to pick you up. Up. Up."* Then pick him up.

Play the wake-up game with an alarm clock (manually wound clocks work best, because they vibrate more). Set the alarm to go off in a few seconds or longer. When you hear/feel the alarm, sign or say, *"Wake-up!"* Point to your ear and to the alarm. Let your child feel the ringing by touching the clock.

At bedtime, hold out your child's bottle, story book or pyjamas. Wait for him to look at you. Then say/sign, *"Bedtime. Bottle. Read book. Pajamas on."* If he doesn't look at you, try doing something funny like pretending to put his pyjamas on yourself, or giving his bottle to the teddy bear, or becoming the friendly bedtime monster.

Establish routines that signal waking up, napping, and bedtime. Routines include putting on and removing hearing equipment, changing clothes, brushing teeth, having snacks, singing rhymes and reading books. When these routines are consistently done in the same order each time, the transition becomes increasingly smooth and predictable. With established routines, there is an opportunity to show flexibility when there are late-night events or lazy weekend mornings. You are modelling personal responsibility when you explain the reason for any exception — along with the reminder that afterwards it will be the same routine as usual.

With older children, use a calendar time in the morning and/or evening whenever you have more time in the routine. Let your child put stickers on special days and cross off each day when it's over. Together you can use a simple drawing to show events: For example, say, *"Let's draw the big doors at the hospital, because tomorrow we go to see Suzanne. She will hook up your processor to her computer. You will be able to show us when you hear the computer beep!"*

Brush your teeth together. Let your young child help put the toothpaste on and brush your teeth, then you have a turn helping her.

Literacy Bonus: Make *"book time"* part of every night's bedtime routine. Read *Goodnight Moon* by Margaret Wise Brown or other books that lull your child into sleepy time.

Changing Diapers and Toileting

Words/Signs to Use for Diapers and Toileting

bathroom	Kleenex	tissue
bottom	mirror	toilet
change	off	toilet paper
clean	on	wait
diaper	pee	wash
dry	poop	washroom
finish	potty	water
flush	sink	wet
help	soap	wipe

- It's important to keep talking while going through these routines. The reason: take advantage of the time spent with your child during this routine to promote listening and communication. Prepare your child to be more independent with toileting, and educate her about body science at the same time.

  Describe your child's action and behaviours leading up to the toileting routine so that your child can communicate what he feels before he needs to go! For example, some children may become restless, cross their legs, look for privacy, etc.

Toileting provides opportunities to model when privacy is appropriate. Show your child how to advocate for herself by closing the bathroom door and saying, *"I need privacy."* Expect her and others to knock on a closed door (and to stamp on the floor if necessary) before entering. This can also turn into a meaningful listening and auditory-awareness activity.

- While you're changing your child's diapers, try a few finger-play stories. Move your fingertips in a circular motion on his palm as you say, *"Round and round the garden goes the little mouse."* Then run your fingers up and down his arm, saying, *"One step, two steps, and* (as you tickle him under the arm) *into his little house he goes!"* or say, *"Round and Round the garden, goes the Teddy Bear! One step, two steps, tickle under there!"*

Again, with your fingertips, playfully tap on your child's tummy. As you tap, say the sound, *"buh, buh, buh."* Then, still using your fingertips, draw circles on your child's tummy. This time say, *"ahhhh"* as you draw circles.

Whenever you change your child's diaper, notice what catches his attention. If he's watching the mobile over his head, talk about this: *"Around and around. Animals go around. There's the cow. Cow says 'moo.'"*

Put an unbreakable mirror near the changing table so your child can look at himself while you talk about his body parts: *"Here's your toes. Wiggle your toes. Wipe your tummy."*

If your child points to his wet diaper or to his pants to let you know that he needs a change or needs to use the toilet, you can say or sign, *"pee."* Then change his diaper or show him to the toilet. If he's beginning to use one- or two-word phrases, such as *"Moses pee,"* you can expand his language by saying, *"Yes, Moses went pee. Yeah! Pee in the toilet!"*

Literacy Bonus: Sing the alphabet song while changing your baby. Before your child washes his hands after toileting, show him the *"H"* for *"hot"* and the *"C"* for *"cold"* on the tap. If your toddler is waiting for a bowel movement, provide him with a small book he can hold, or look at a book together while supervising him.

Bathtime

Words/Signs to Use at Bathtime

alligator	*dry*	*soap*
bathtub	*duck*	*splash*
blow	*fish*	*turtle*
bubbles	*frog*	*towel*
careful	*hot/cold*	*wash*
clean	*in/out*	*water*
clothes off	*pour*	*wet*
dirty	*shampoo*	*your*
drip	*slipper*	

Words/Signs to Use in Describing the Body

back	*face*	*knee*
cheek	*feet*	*leg*
chin	*hair*	*mouth*
ears	*hands*	*nose*
eyes	*head*	*toe*

Describe what you're doing as you prepare your child's bath: *"Put the plug in. Turn the water on. Uh, oh, the water is hot! We need more cold water."* Always tell your child before you actually do anything. Obviously, once his hearing device is off, this is not an ideal time to work on listening skills. But it can be a good time to practice signing and meaningful facial expressions and gestures.

If you're using sign, name your child's body parts as you wash him. (If your child has some degree of hearing, an enjoyable way to teach body parts is to sing a little song, *"This is the way we wash your . . . "* as you name each part.) Once your child is able to do so, encourage him to name his own body parts as he helps you wash.

While you're signing, remember to keep the length of your phrases or sentences just slightly longer than those he is using. If he's not yet using real signs, then you should use one- to three-word phrases. If he is already signing in phrases that combine four or five signs, then you can use six to eight signs in a sentence.

Here are examples of three language levels: (1) *"Wash hair."* (2) *"Wash long hair."* (3) *"I'm washing your hair with Daddy's shampoo."*

To assist your child in understanding concepts — for instance, cause and effect, as well as the function of different activities — explain what you're doing and what's happening: *"Your feet are dirty. We'll wash them. Now they're clean. Oh! Soap in your eyes. Ow, that hurts! Rinse the soap out. Now your eyes feel better. No soap in your eyes."*

Talk about the fun activities that are happening in the bathtub: *"You're splashing! Splash the water!"*

If your child is already using more advanced language, you can begin introducing concepts like float or sink. Tell him which bath toys float and which sink. You can also talk about the number of toys in the tub (two ducks) and the size of toys (big duck, little duck).

Encourage your child to help you wash a toy doll in the tub. Talk about what you're doing. As you dry your child, play peek-a-boo with the towel.

Use some of the same bathtime toys and songs during your indoor play routines when your child is wearing his hearing equipment. This way, he may learn the sounds associated with the songs and toys, which he could not hear before.

If you have a video/DVD camera, you can also video tape your bathtime routine. Then, while your child is wearing his hearing device, you can watch the video tape/DVD together and discuss the same activities.

Use foam or plastic letters and numbers designed for water play.

Encourage your child to do what he can for himself to increase his independence.

Literacy Bonus:

- Use letters and numbers made for water play. While bathing your child, practice the alphabet — arrange numbers in order and spell familiar words.

- Use books about bathtime before and after bathing (when your child's hearing device is on) to reinforce vocabulary and concepts related to the bathing routine.

- Borrow or buy books about body science and sexual health, which make it easier to teach real names for private body parts.

*I can say "uuuup" when
I pull up pants or socks
to help my child associate
sounds with actions.*

Getting Dressed and Undressed

Words/Signs to Use for Dressing and Undressing

belt	*inside*	*shoes*
boots	*jeans*	*shorts*
button	*long*	*sock*
closet	*mittens*	*sweater*
clothes	*off / on*	*tights*
coat/jacket	*pants*	*umbrella*
cold	*pull*	*under*
drawer	*push*	*underwear*
dress	*put*	*warm*
glove	*scarf*	*zipper*
hat	*shirt*	

Talk about what you and your child are doing. For example:

- *"Pull. Pull socks off. Lift your arms up. Arms up. Lift arms up."*

- *"I'm brushing your hair. Here's the brush. You're helping. You're brushing your hair. You look beautiful now."*

Every time you help your child change clothes, use the words *"on"* and *"off"* to describe what you do with each item of clothing. You can say and/or sign two-word phrases over and over again: *"Shirt off. Shoes on."*

If your child is just starting to talk and/or sign in single words, he may imitate you by saying, *"On"* as he tries to put his shoes on. You can help increase his vocabulary by adding one or two words to whatever he says or signs. For instance:

- Your child says, *"On."* You say, *"Shoes on. One shoe on. Two shoes on."*

- Your child signs, *"Sock."* You say/sign, *"Yes, sock on. Put sock on. White sock."*

- Your child says, *"Boot off."* You say/sign, *"Take your boot off. Two boots off."*

If your child enjoys songs, as you put on each item of clothing you can sing, *"This is the way we put on our . . ."* (to the tune of *"Here We Go Round the Mulberry Bush"*). When you get to the name of that item, pause, hold up the clothing, and wait for your child to say/sign his name. Then pull on that piece of clothing. As his language ability grows, leave off more words at the end for him to fill in.

Talk/sign about the colours of your child's clothing (a red dress) and the numbers (two socks, one shirt).

Give your child appropriate choices about what he puts on that are also acceptable to you. For example: *"Do you want pants or shorts?"*

To help with the morning routine, choose clothes the night before; and lay them out for the morning. Include your child in the decision-making process, and describe what you expect in the morning. For example: *"You picked out your socks all by yourself! When you wake up, we'll put your undershirt and cochlear implant on together. Then you can finish dressing yourself with the clothes on your bed!"*

Here are examples of words and phrases you can use when giving choices to your child.

Literacy Bonus: Help your child associate certain sounds with specific movements and actions when she gets dressed or undressed. Say, *"uuuup"* while pulling pants and socks up, emphasizing the *"p"* sound at the end. Say, *"zzzzzzip"* whenever zipping a zipper. When you emphasize sounds and pull the sounds in words apart by saying them slowly and separately, you are helping your child pay attention to the individual sounds in words and their place in the word — beginning, middle or end. This develops **phonemic awareness,** which is important for reading readiness.

Cooking

Words/Signs to Use: What We Do in the Kitchen

bake	*find*	*scrub*
boil	*finish*	*shake*
bring	*get*	*shut*
careful	*help*	*sprinkle*
cook	*hold*	*squeeze*
cut	*measure*	*stir*
don't touch!	*mix*	*taste*
drink	*open*	*wait*
drip	*peel*	*wash*
dry	*pour*	*wipe*

Words/Signs to Use: Things We Use in the Kitchen

bowl	*pan*	*stove*
can	*pot*	*sugar*
cup	*recipe*	*table*
mixer	*refrigerator*	*toaster*
oven	*spoon*	

Words/Signs to Use: Descriptive Words

all gone	little	sticky
big	ready	sweet
cold	round	thick
enough	salty	warm
fast	same	wet
full	sharp	
hot	sour	

Even young children can participate in cooking chores. When brothers and sisters want to help pour and stir, this offers many opportunities for turn-taking. Ask: *"Whose turn?"* Encourage your deaf or hard of hearing child to say, *"My turn."* Or, *"Amy's turn."* Or, *"Mommy's turn."*

Name the food, equipment, and activities that are involved in preparing a meal. Emphasize words and ideas appropriate for your child's language level. If he is just beginning to talk, he may be ready to learn the word milk. For a more advanced talker/signer, words like cutting board are appropriate.

In preparing lunch, describe for your child what you're doing. Say, *"Time for lunch. Stir the soup. Cook. Get the bowls. Pour. Taste the soup."*

If you have a blender, hot air popcorn popper, or other noisy appliance, you can use it to alert your child to a variety of sounds. Before your turn the appliance on, prepare your child by telling him to *"listen"* and point to your ear. Use the words, on, off, stop, go to indicate the presence and absence of sound. If it's safe to do so, let him feel the appliance vibrating.

You can increase your child's vocabulary by repeating what he has said and then adding a few more words of your own. For example: Your child says, *"Hot."* You can say, *"Hot stove. Be careful! Stove is hot!"*

Your child says, *"Milk spilled."* You can add, *"The milk spilled on the table. That's OK. Wipe the milk off."*

Your child says, *"Pour flour in."* You extend this with, *"Pour the flour in the bowl. Two cups of flour in."*

Literacy Bonus: Cooking and preparing food includes following recipes and directions. Listening to the steps you describe that are required to make a dish strengthens memory and sequencing abilities, both critical for reading. Even eating an apple can be broken down into a few simple steps that your baby can follow: *"First we get the apple from the fridge. Where is the apple? There it is!"* Then, *"We wash the apple. Listen — water on. Washing, washing . . . all clean!"* Finally, *"Now we cut the apple. Cut, cut, cut. Careful . . . sharp! All done! One, two, three, four pieces of apple. Mmmm, so good!"*

Use picture-recipe books with toddlers and preschoolers. Try making cookies with alphabet and number cookie cutters.

Mealtime

Words/Signs to Use at Mealtime: Food

apple	*french fries*	*popcorn*
applesauce	*grapes*	*popsicle*
banana	*gum*	*potato*
beans	*hamburger*	*potato chip*
bread	*ice*	*pudding*
butter	*fish*	*pickles*
cake	*ice cream*	*pizza*
candy	*Jell-O*	*pumpkin*
carrots	*juice*	*raisin*
cereal	*lollipop*	*sandwich*
cheese	*meat*	*soda pop*
chicken	*melon*	*soup*
chocolate	*milk*	*spaghetti*
coffee	*muffin*	*strawberry*
cookie	*noodles*	*toast*
corn	*nuts*	*tuna*
cracker	*orange*	*vitamins*
donut	*pancake*	*water*
drink	*peanut butter*	*yogurt*
egg	*peas*	

Other Mealtime Words

all gone	*finished*	*more*
bib	*fork*	*plate*
bottle	*good*	*sit*
bowl	*highchair*	*snack*
breakfast	*hungry*	*spoon*
cup	*kitchen*	*supper*
dinner	*knife*	*table*
drink	*like*	*thirsty*
eat	*lunch*	*want*

Observe your child's nonverbal behaviour — his facial and body expressions, gestures, and actions. Try to detect what he is thinking or feeling and make appropriate comments, like these: *"You want down."* Or, *"You are a hungry boy!"* Or, *"More milk?"* Or, *"All gone."* Or, *"Drink juice."* Or, *"Bang, bang goes the spoon."* Or, *"Mmmm, good cereal."* Or *"No more. Finished."*

Describe the food you're eating: hot, cold, sweet or sour.

Talk about the food you're preparing for a specific meal. Repeat the words several times before you put the meal on the table. For example: *"See broccoli. Put the broccoli in the pan. It's cooking. The broccoli is hot!"* Then, when your serve it, you could say, *"Here's your broccoli. Oh, yummy green broccoli."* When your child has finished his meal, again name the food he ate. *"You ate your potatoes and your broccoli."*

Here are examples of words and phrases you can use when giving choices to your child.

NUMBER OF SYLLABLES		
1	2	3
cone	apple	banana
fries	butter	hamburger
jam	cookie	ice-cream cone
juice	french fries	Mc Nuggets
milk	honey	peanut butter
salt	pizza	
	popcorn	
	snack time	

Don't force your child to imitate your words yet. But if he voluntarily imitates you, add a word or two and repeat these back to him. For example: Your child says, *"Hot."* You might say, *"Hot muffin." Your child says, "Pour milk."* You respond with, *"Pour milk in the bowl."* Your child says, *" Egg spilled on floor."* You expand that with, *"Oh, the egg spilled on the clean floor. It slipped out of my hand."*

Try putting your child's hearing device on before mealtime as a consistent routine. When children are distracted by mealtime activities and busy eating, they're less likely to be aware of the hearing device.

Stand by your child's chair or highchair, and get his attention. To help focus your child, first alert him to listen before you use any sounds that you want him to hear. (At mealtime, always be aware of sticky foods and liquids that could be destructive to hearing devices.)

Babies and toddlers love to feed others. Encourage turn-taking by letting your child feed you, too.

Literacy Bonus: Use mealtimes, when you are sitting together, to build story comprehension and storytelling skills. These narrative skills are important for your child to be able to read and construct stories — both necessary for academic achievement. Start building these skills early by talking about the day's events and happenings at mealtimes. If your child is an infant, telling a story about the day in a sing-song, captivating voice will keep his interest. Pause between each event to peak his curiosity. Involve your older child by modelling and prompting him to participate in going over the day's activities. For example: say, *"After we had breakfast, I brushed my teeth and went to work."* Then give your child a turn to tell his version. End by taking turns telling what the highlights and disappointments of the day were. Sharing your experiences also benefits the relationship you build with your child.

Washing Dishes

Words/Signs to Use While Washing Dishes

bowl	*fork*	*splash*
bubbles	*glass*	*spoon*
cup	*knife*	*wash*
dirty	*plate*	*wet*
dishcloth	*soap*	*wipe*
dry		

It's nearly impossible to have eye contact with your child when you're washing dishes — since you're both facing the sink. Instead, try to get his attention in other ways. Pause or stop the action until he looks at you. Call his name. Or tap him gently.

Let's suppose one of you has just broken a dish. Your child says, *"Broken!"* To help increase his language, you might add, *"Dish is broken. Dish fell and broke. Mommy will fix it."*

Your child is playing with bubbles in the sink. He says, *"Bubble all gone."* You can say, *"The bubble is all gone. Bubble went pop."*

Literacy Bonus: Count the number of dirty dishes. Talk about how many dishes there are to clean as you put them in the dishwasher, or how many are left as you put them away. Counting is also a literacy event, because it leads to written mathematical equations. Familiarity with vocabulary about quantity (for example, many, few, and none) facilitates math learning early on.

Housekeeping

Words/Signs to Use

broom / mop	*garden*	*plant*
clean	*grass*	*put away*
clean up	*hose*	*rake leaves*
dirty	*laundry*	*sweep*
dust	*lawn mower*	*tools*
fix	*messy*	*vacuum*
garage	*pick up garbage*	*washing machine*

Encourage your child to help with housekeeping chores during the day. Young children benefit from having daily responsibilities — putting their dirty clothes in the laundry or setting the table. Independence builds confidence and self-esteem. If possible, have a few child-sized tools (broom, shovel, hammer) so your child can *"work"* along with you. Name each tool. Talk about what you're doing, thinking and feeling.

Take turns with simple household tasks: loading or unloading the dishwasher, one item at a time; putting socks in a drawer, one pair at a time, etc. Needless to say, it takes longer to complete housework this way. But by including your child in such chores you're teaching him valuable skills and building his self-esteem, as well as his sense of usefulness in your family.

While you work, use the sounds around you for listening games. Get your child's attention. Then point to an appliance (for instance: washer, dryer, vacuum) and tell him, *"Listen!"* Turn the appliance on. Talk about the sound: *"It's loud,"* or *"It's noisy."* Sometimes let your child turn the appliance on, and have him feel its vibrations. But, remember, it will be difficult for him to understand your speech when there is background noise from appliances. This is a good time to practice signing and speech reading.

If your child frequently tries to communicate with you over background noise, you can show him how to make communication better. Say/sign *"It's too noisy. I can't hear you. Wait"* Eliminate the noise and say, *"That's better. Now I can hear you. What do you want to tell me?"*

Literacy Bonus: Count how many place settings there are. Write names out for each place setting to show who sits where.

Reading and Writing Activities

Sit face-to-face with your child and position yourself so that he can see the book and your face and hands at the same time. Give him a few moments to look at the pictures and words and then your face. Wait to tell the story until he's watching you. (To keep his attention on your face, you may want to turn the book over while you talk.) Once your child has enough language or knows the story well, try telling parts of it before you show him a picture. To free your hands for signing, use a clear, plastic cookbook stand.

Whenever your child sees you reading or writing, he's learning a lot about literacy. If you're writing a letter, reading a newspaper, the mail, or a recipe, call your child's attention to what you're doing. Explain, *"I'm writing a letter to grandma."* Or, *"I'm reading an interesting story in the newspaper."*

Any caption for this illustration?

Begin reading to your child when he is a baby. At first, give him plastic or laminated cardboard books. Encourage him to an active participant by reading books that he can touch and feel. *Pat the Bunny* by Dorothy Kunhardt is a favorite with many babies. Books with easy, familiar words and clear illustrations are best. Read the same books again and again. Try different ways to tell the same story: use stick or finger puppets or props to act out a story like *The Three Bears*. Tell the story in your own words. (Change or add words to match sounds your child is learning.) Then, let your child tell you the story in his words.

Alter your voice often when you tell a story. Use a low, gruff voice for the big, bad wolf. Use a high squeaky voice for the three little pigs. Slow your voice down in anticipation, and then pause before you turn the page. Use dramatic facial and body expressions.

Look for books that talk about *"noises"* and *"sounds"* and those that play with words — like the Dr. Seuss books. Point to pictures and make appropriate sounds as you read the story. If someone in the story is beating a drum, you can say, *"Boom, boom, boom."* For a fish in the story, say *"Glub, glub."* For a bubble, say *"Pop!"*

Consider other ways to assist your child in learning letters, numbers and words. Magnetic letters and numbers, computer games, and alphabet cookie cutters are a few of the toys that encourage early reading and writing. Wherever you see words and numbers — on items in your home, or on posters, signs, etc. when you're out driving or walking — point them out to your child.

I can help my child learn to read by pointing out numbers and letters around us.

Art

Words/Signs to Use: Art

beautiful	*nice*	*scissors*
chalk	*paper*	*shape*
circle	*picture*	*smooth*
colour	*Play-Doh*	*square*
crayons	*press*	*sticks*
cut	*pretty*	*sticker*
draw	*rectangle*	*sticky*
glue	*roll*	*tape*
good work	*rough*	*triangle*

Words/Signs to Use: Colours

black	*grey*	*red*
blue	*orange*	*white*
brown	*pink*	*yellow*
green	*purple*	

Most children love to draw or paint. Art work of every kind offers a great opportunity to add new words to your child's vocabulary.

Encourage your child to describe his own drawings and paintings, and then print the words he says to label pictures or tell the story. Build self-esteem by reminding the artist to sign his creation.

Use drawings to illustrate a sequence of events. For example: Use the colouring book provided by the cochlear implant manufacturer that tells about going to the hospital for the implant surgery.

When you're using a paintbrush, felt marker or crayons, match your drawing or painting to your voice. Use a loud voice as you make large or thick strokes. Use a soft voice as you draw thin lines. Make long sounds, *"Ahhhhhhhh"* for long, continuous movements. Make abrupt sounds, *"Dot, dot, dot"* to go with short movements. Use sounds your child can easily imitate.

Making your own books is another good way to reinforce language learning. Use stickers, stamps and pictures from magazines. Real objects — like leaves or bird feathers — are good, too. Let your child add ideas and drawings about his own experiences. Share these with family and friends to help them better understand his attempts at communication.

Go to the library on a routine basis. Public library programs include story times and reading clubs.

Literacy Bonus: Let your child tell you about her creation. If she describes it with sounds, words, or signs write those on her art to label her work. Make sure she puts her name on her work. Her printed name is then associated with pride, ownership, and a positive literacy experience.

AT PLAY

Indoor Play

Words/Signs to Use: Indoor Play

1, 2, 3	*letter*	*pretend*
ABC	*list*	*put*
airplane	*listen*	*puzzle*
ball	*little*	*read*
balloon	*make*	*shake*
blocks	*my turn*	*share*
boat	*name*	*small*
book	*number*	*spell*
build	*on / off*	*story*
car	*open*	*toys away*
close	*paint*	*train*
doll	*paper*	*truck*
dress up	*patty cake*	*up / down*
drive	*peek-a-boo*	*word*
fall down	*pen*	*write*
fire truck	*pencil*	*your turn*
game	*picture*	
help	*play*	

- Be a play partner, not a teacher. Let your child take the lead. At first, just sit and wait. Then, imitate what he's doing or saying.

- Match your words to your child's interest and play. For example: You and your child are taking turns rolling a ball across the floor. Suddenly, he stops, holds the ball, and looks closely at it. You may be tempted to keep the turns going by directing him to *"Roll the ball."* Instead, watch and wait. Try to guess why your child has stopped and what he's thinking. Let's say he found some gum stuck on the ball. You could say, *"Oh, gum! You found gum. Gum stuck on the ball. Ooooh, that's sticky. Yuck. It's stuck to your finger now. You don't like that."*

- Put a few toys in a cloth bag, an old sock or a box. Bring the toys out one at a time. Say the sound for each toy: *"Woof,"* for a toy dog, *"Mmmmm,"* for an airplane. Put the toys in front of your child. As he picks up a toy, again say the appropriate sound. Talk about what your child is doing with each toy.

- Once he's familiar with the sounds, try saying the sound before he picks up the toy to see if he can match the sounds he hears with the right toy. Start with two sounds that are very different — *"Vroom, vroom"* for a car, *"Hop, hop, hop"* for a rabbit. Later, add more sounds. When your child is familiar with this listening game and ready for a greater challenge, you can use sounds that are more alike: *"Moo"* for a cow and *"Boo"* for a ghost.

Taking time to play with my child means fun and learning for both of us.

- Let your child make a sound, and you pick up the toy for the sound he makes. You can try picking up the wrong toy to see if he'll catch your "mistake."

Here are some other ways to expand your child's vocabulary during playtime:

- Your child points to a story book and asks, *"Book?"* You pick it up, open the pages, and say, *"Read a book."*

- *"Play ball,"* your child urges. You toss him the ball and expand his message: *"Play ball with Mommy."*

- Fitting a small doll into his toy truck, your child says, *"Man truck." "Yes,"* you tell him, *"man goes in the truck."*

- Your child is playing with a toy cow. *"Cow big eat,"* he says. You help supply details (and increase his language) with this: *"The big cow eats grass."*

- Singing or signing songs is an enjoyable way to listen or watch for different sounds and words. Once your child has established some favourite songs, give him time to anticipate what comes next in a song. For example, in the song Old Macdonald Had a Farm, wait a moment after you sing, *"ee, i, ee, i …"* and give him a chance to add the *"oh."* In Ring Around the Rosies, sign *"We all fall …."* Then wait for him to add *"down."* When you play this game, be sure to show excitement and anticipation in your face and voice.

Literacy Bonus: Encourage confidence in hearing and processing language through listening. Sit side by side or behind your child when you are reading to him.

Outdoor Play

Words/Signs to Use During Outdoor Play

ant	*hit*	*spider*
bat	*jump*	*star*
beach	*moon*	*stick*
bee	*outside*	*street*
bicycle	*park*	*stroller*
bug	*rain*	*sun*
butterfly	*rock*	*swing*
camping	*run*	*teeter totter*
careful	*sand*	*tent*

catch	*sandbox*	*tree*
caterpillar	*shovel*	*wagon*
climb	*sky*	*wait*
dig	*slide*	*walk*
flower	*snow*	*wind*
football	*snowsuit*	*yard*
go / stop	*snowman*	

- The great outdoors provides many different listening experiences. If you're worried about your child losing his hearing aids when he's outside, try attaching the aids to his clothing with fishing wire or a glasses strap and a safety pin. (See Chapter 3, Hearing Aids: Putting Them On.)

- Alert your child to the sounds around him: *"Listen, an airplane."* Or, *"I hear an ambulance."* Or, *"There's a dog barking. That's loud!"* If your child is at a distance from you and out of listening range, you'll need to bring him closer before he can hear you.

- Make sounds with natural objects you see and find: bang sticks together, listen to the rocks "plunk" in the creek, crunch leaves underfoot.

- Whenever your child is outside playing, you'll find it helpful to use broad expressions and gestures to get his attention. Bring your arms toward your body to show him *"Come here."* Shake your head or nod vigorously, frown or smile to show, *"No"* or *"Yes."*

- On the swings, stop each time you've given your child a push and wait for him to let you know he wants another push. For instance, he may say/sign, *"more," "swing"* or *"push."* If he vocalizes, cries, or does nothing after 10 seconds, model what you believe he's thinking. Say / sign, *"More, more swing!"* or *"Push, you want push!"* Build in the expectation for your child to communicate by saying *"1, 2, 3....go!"* when you are getting ready to push the swing or when he goes down the slide. Pause after *"3."* Wait to see if your child will say *"Go!"* He may enjoy the anticipation and count together with you, too.

- Associate your child's actions with sounds that match: *"Wheee,"* as he goes down the slide. *"Hop, hop, hop,"* as he jumps. *"Uuuup, Dowwwwn,"* as you push him high on the swing. Remember: make your voice interesting to listen to.

- *"Me go down,"* your child says grinning with pleasure as he zips down the slide. You can respond with, *"You go down the slide. I go down the slide, too."* Describing his ride, he tells you, *"Slide go fast."* You can say, *"You went fast down the slide."*

Outdoor play gives me lots of opportunities to match sound and words to my child's actions.

- On the merry-go-round, if your child says, *"Go!"* you can add, *"Go around and around."* After a while, let's suppose your child begins to feel dizzy. But he's not sure how to let you know. He says, *"No, no!"* You understand what he's trying to tell you, and you give him the words he needs: *"No More. Stop merry-go-round. You want off."*

- Imitate your child's actions and enjoyment of the outdoors. Observe what he's interested in so that you can prepare signed and spoken vocabulary words to learn together during outdoor play experiences.

Summer is full of wonderful sounds, but the outdoors can be hard on a hearing device! Help your child with summer hearing device care. Here is a checklist you and your child can use:

___ I can take care of my hearing device.

___ I keep my hearing device out of the hot sun (not on the dash of the car).

___ I keep my hearing device out of the water.

___ I protect my hearing device from sand at the beach.

___ I have a special container to protect my hearing device.

___ I have a special place that this container is kept.

___ I keep the tubing clear of moisture (watch for those little bubbles!).

___ I have a drying kit to put the hearing device in overnight.

Literacy Bonus: Be nature detectives and inspect everything outdoors! Look for bugs in the garden, crabs at the beach, and birds in the forest. Curiosity about nature translates into a wealth of new vocabulary, making reading those familiar, printed words much easier.

Follow up on a day outdoors with a book about the weather: *The Snowy Day* by Ezra Jack Keats or *Zoe's Rainy Day* by Barbara Reid. For a book about gardening, read *The Carrot Seed* by Ruth Krauss. If your child is fascinated by bugs, try *The Very Hungry Caterpillar* by Eric Carle. A fine child's book about outdoor places is *Over In the Meadow* by Ezra Jack Keats.

Entertainment

Words/Signs to Use: Entertainment

CD-ROM	*loud*	*screen*
computer	*movie*	*TV*
dark	*music*	*talk*
DVD	*pop*	*telephone*
games	*popcorn*	*video*
hear	*quiet*	*video/remote control*
listen	*radio*	*watch*
look		

- Many families display the captioning on the TV screen. Although your child may not yet know how to read, captioning can help him learn that written symbols have meaning and that they are as important to watch as the picture. Seeing the words gives him practice with letter and word recognition.

- If your family enjoys watching television programs and movies, prepare your child ahead of time for what the show will be about. You may have to invent sign names for characters in the show. After a movie, discuss what happened. Walt Disney animated shows are popular, because they have a lot of action and visual information.

- You can borrow children's videos or DVD's from the library long enough to watch them several times. Put the video on, and pause occasionally to see if your child can predict what will happen next. If he's older and is familiar with the movie, encourage him to retell the story with words and pictures. You can help him by asking, *"Tell me what happened when . . ."* Or prompt him with something like this: *"First, Goldilocks ate all the porridge. Then what did she do?"* Ask, *"What was your favourite part?"* Or, *"What happened that was scary?"* Get the books, audio-taped books, music / story CD's and CD-ROM's that go along with the movies.

- Many signed videos are now available for deaf and hard of hearing children. Your child will enjoy these videos, because she can begin to understand the story through real language.

- Listening to music that is both loud and low-pitched is a good way to encourage your child to pay attention to sound. Before you turn the music on, alert her to listen by pointing to your ear, then to the speakers or radio. When you turn the music on, make sure the volume is already turned up. Use facial expressions to show surprise at the loud sounds. It's fun to dance with your child (hold her or join hands) until the music stops.

Literacy Bonus: Read the book together before watching the movie. Many popular children's movies are based on books or have the book version.

Family Events And Holidays

Words/Signs to Use for Special Days

birthday	*open*	*tomorrow*
candy	*party*	*tonight*
celebrate	*present*	*visit*
day	*remember*	*wedding*
excited	*surprise*	*when*
funeral	*thank you*	*will*
happy	*tired*	*year*
holiday	*today*	*yesterday*
month		

- Like all children, your young one will enjoy participating in the special events and holidays that are part of family life. Use pictures that he can paste in a scrapbook and real objects — like Christmas ornaments — to help him understand and look forward to these memorable times. A calendar with simple stick figures or special stickers can also help him to visualize coming events. Cross off the days as you count down to the big occasion. In time, your child will begin to see a pattern of events: *"My birthday is before Christmas. First comes Easter, then Mother's Day."*

- When you have a children's party, play a game that involves sound awareness like "Musical Chairs." Bang a drum or play music as the children walk around a line of chairs. When the music stops, encourage them to say/sign, *"Stop!"* and to find a chair. Before you start the music again, say/sign *"Listen!"* To reduce competition, even though you take away chairs, allow all the children to keep playing until everyone ends up sitting on one chair when the sound stops. "Hot Potato" is another good game involving sound. Pass a ball around a circle until the music stops. The child still holding the ball has the "hot potato." Another version of this game is a trinket or treat wrapped in layers of paper. Each time the music stops, the child holding the item peels off a layer.

- Birthday parties involve many traditional activities like blowing out candles on the cake and singing *"Happy Birthday"* — a great song for children to sing and sign, because it's simple and repetitive. This is also an easy song for adults to learn to sign. Encourage your child to sing along with the family.

- Whenever you decorate your home with a holiday theme, talk about what you're doing. When your child adds his own comments, expand on what he says.

- Holidays are a great time to bring your baby's awareness to interesting sounds, smells, and flavours of traditional foods. Bells, music, fireworks, and other noises fill the air. Toddlers are motivated to try different sounds, such as *"puh puh puh,"* and other ways of forming their lips to blow out candles (carefully!). Tasting and smelling different treats and aromas can lead to *"mmmm"* or *"yucky!"*

- When a large group of family members gather, it can be overwhelming for a deaf or hard of hearing child to follow conversations with unfamiliar people — especially when there's a lot of background noise. Well ahead of time, show your child pictures

of the people who'll be there. If your child uses sign,
give each family member a name sign, based on a
distinguishing characteristic: Grandpa John has a
big beard; Uncle Jim has a loud voice. Use the first
letter of each person's name.

Here are examples of words and phrases you can use when
giving choices to your child.

- When your child is talking/signing with family
  members, help him out by demonstrating some
  basic signs to them ahead of time. Tell them what
  your child is saying/signing. Also, interpret
  key words of a conversation for your child. Let
  family members know that miming, gesturing,
  drawing, and showing are all important ways
  to communicate. Even if they don't know sign
  language. Include your child as much as possible in
  everything that's said, and encourage others to do
  the same. This way, your child develops a sense of
  belonging to his extended family.

Literacy Bonus: Before a traditional holiday, borrow books
about it from the library. Put up decorations that have the
written words naming the holiday or celebration.

AWAY FROM HOME

Many parents are anxious about drawing attention
to their family in public. Stares from strangers may
trigger emotions about their child with the hearing loss.
Many parents describe feeling hurt, embarrassed and
protective in these situations. Hearing devices and visual
communication may be noticed by curious strangers.
Be prepared with responses. Discuss how you and your
family would like to approach questions from people.
If you feel that you might cry if anyone asks about your

child, you may decide to have a supportive friend or family member with you who can encourage you to get through it.

- Remember that how you give (or avoid giving) information about your child's hearing loss, his hearing device, and communication strategies in the presence of your child, will be the way your child gives information himself. Usually, a simple explanation is sufficient.

- For example: *"Tommy wears hearing aids because without them, he doesn't hear some soft high pitched sounds. The hearing aids work best when you get close to him and talk normally."* Or, *"My daughter is learning to listen with a cochlear implant. It is a device that provides her with hearing sensation, since she was born deaf."*

Shopping

Words/Signs to Use While Shopping

buy	*how much?*	*purse*
cents	*list*	*shopping*
dollars	*money*	*store*
food	*pay*	*wallet*

- If your child says/signs, *"store"* when you go shopping, you can expand his language by adding the names of stores and what you buy there: *"We're going to a hardware store. We buy things for building there. We need some nails for hammering."* If your child is using signs, you may have to finger-spell some words like "hardware" until you learn or invent a sign for this. Some English words need to be spelled out if you want to use the exact word.

- If your child says, *"In"* as he helps you put food into the basket, you can add, *"In the basket. Put the food in the basket."*

- He sets a quart of milk in your shopping cart and signs, *"Cold."* You nod agreement and sign/say *"Yes, cold milk."*

- Your child points to her favourite cereal and says, *"Uh."* You tell her, *"Cheerios. Want Cheerios. You want Cheerios."*

- Perhaps she asks, *"Where ice cream?"* You can fill in with, *"Where is the ice cream?"* Then extend this by adding, *"Ice cream is cold. It's in the freezer."*

- Include your child in gift giving. Shop together and make cards at home. Your child's art and his attempt at signing his own name encourages literacy and teaches the value of self-expression and the gift of giving.

Literacy Bonus: When you're going to the grocery store, help your child make a list of items you'll need, using store flyers or pictures from magazines. Take a pen along, and let your child check off each item on the list as you buy it.

Community Outings and Trips

Words/Signs to Use: Outings

bathing suit	*gas station*	*parade*
car	*gym*	*picnic*
circus	*jump*	*police station*
clown	*keys*	*policeman/ woman*
downtown	*letter*	*restaurant*
empty	*library*	*ride*
fill	*mail*	*seatbelt*
fire station	*mail carrier*	*stamp*
firefighter	*motorcycle*	*swim*
gas	*museum*	*swimming pool*

- Deaf and hard of hearing children are often unaware of plans for a coming trip, because they may not overhear the conversations around them. It's important to help your child understand what is going to happen. You can involve him in planning an outing by showing him a picture (a photograph or drawing) of the place where he'll be going or the people he will see.

Literacy Bonus: Keep a calendar of events for your child. Draw or paste a picture of each special event that will occur during the month. You might post a picture of a hearing aid, for instance, on the day you take your child to the audiologist. Reading a calendar promotes literacy and helps you keep organized.

At a Farm or Zoo: Animals

Words/Signs to Use

bear	duck	horse
bird	elephant	lamb / sheep
bunny	fish	monkey
cat	frog	mouse
chicken	gerbil	penguin
cow	giraffe	pig
dog	hamster	rabbit

- Make animal sounds. These are some of the first sounds babies make.

- Children love animals. Investigate where different animals live and what they eat in books about animals at the library.

- Find out what your child's favourite animal is.

- Talk about the kinds of animals you see in cartoons, movies, and books.

Literacy Bonus: Visit a farm and read the signs or brochure about the animals.

At the Audiologist's

Words/Signs to Use

circle time	*hearing aids*	*snack time*
cochlear implant	*listen*	*speech processor*
computer	*loud*	*take turns*
computer	*mapping*	*teacher*
earmolds	*nap time*	*too loud*
FM	*picture (tympanogram)*	*turned on/off*
free play	*preschool*	*type*
friends	*quiet*	*uncomfortable*
game	*school*	*wait*
headphones	*share*	
hear	*show and tell*	

Group-Learning Programs, School, and Daycare

School

- Well before your child begins school, it's a good idea to help him become familiar with the words he may need.

- Visit the school your child will attend. Draw pictures on the calendar to show school days. Take photographs of the classroom and start an album about your child's preschool and school experiences.

- Learn the songs and rhymes that are part of the class routine and themes. Ask the teacher if you can visit to learn the songs, or send a tape recorder record for songs and stories.

- Put together an information package about your child's hearing device. Include answers to frequently asked questions: for example, *"What if the device comes off or is not working?"*

- Encourage your child's independence at home in dealing with his hearing device in preparation for school. Discuss what your child would do if there were problems with the device that interfered with understanding and good communication.

Literacy Bonus: Visit the school library with your child. Find out the librarian's name and what the children do during library time.

A FEW CLOSING WORDS

Recently, we spoke with a mother whose child was diagnosed several years ago as having a severe hearing loss. She told us that in the first two or three years after her son's diagnosis, she was unable to see anything positive about their situation. Yet today, she feels that what seemed a crushing blow at first has been "a journey of discovery" for their whole family.

Together, they have found a whole new world and have become more aware and understanding of people who are different from themselves. They have worked together to learn how best to communicate with each other. They've made new friends with other families and have discovered a strength and confidence inside themselves that they didn't know was there.

As the parent of a deaf or hard of hearing child, you may sometimes feel overwhelmed by the job ahead. But as time passes, you'll gain a fresh self-confidence and find that watching your child grow and develop is both endlessly exciting and deeply satisfying.

As you start on your "journey of discovery," we'll be cheering for you and your family.

HELPFUL RESOURCES

BOOKS

Your Child's Hearing Loss: What Parents Need To Know, by D. Waldman & J. Roush, Ph.D., Penguin Publishing Group, New York, 2005.
Although we purchased many copies of this book for our library, this book rarely sits for long on our shelves because it is so popular with families. This book was co-authored by the parent of a child with a hearing loss and by the director of a Speech and Hearing department at the University of North Carolina.

Not Deaf Enough: Raising A Child Who Is Hard Of Hearing With Hugs, Humor, And Imagination, by P. Candlish, Alexander Graham Bell Association, 1996.
There have been many books written about deaf children but it is often difficult to find a book that focuses on hard of hearing children. It was for this reason that the author, the mother of a hard of hearing child, wrote this excellent book.

Choices In Deafness: A Parents Guide (revised), by S. Schwartz -Editor, Woodbine House, Rockville, MD, 1996.
Choices in Deafness explains the differences between the various communication options and includes interviews with parents who describe the decisions they made.

The Signing Family: What Every Parent Should Know About Sign Communication by D. Stewart & B. Luetke-Stahlman, Washington, DC, Gallaudet University Press, 1998.
This book discusses American Sign Language, Signed English, Seeing Exact English, and Contact Sign and how parents can incorporate sign language into their home.

Baby Talk: Helping Your Hearing Impaired Baby Listen And Talk, by V. Kozak and B. Moog-Brooks, St. Louis, Central Institute for the Deaf, 2001.
This book, written by specialists at the Central Institute for the Deaf, includes tips for parents wanting ideas for helping their child learn to talk.

When Your Child Is Deaf: A Guide For Parents by D. Luterman, York Press, Maryland, 1991.
This is a good book for parents of a newly diagnosed deaf child. David Luterman covers topics such as: coping, parenting a deaf child, hearing testing, hearing aids, and educational and communication choices.

One Mother's Story - Raising Deaf Children: An Educator Becomes A Parent by B. Luetke-Stahlman, Modern Signs Press Inc., Los Alamitos, California, 1996.
All members of this family strive to provide an environment in which audition, speech, language, and socialization skills are developed and Deaf culture is respected.

Alandra's Lilacs: The Story Of A Mother And Her Deaf Daughter by T. Bowers, Washington, DC, Gallaudet University Press, 1999.
This is the story of the journey of Teresa Bowers and her deaf daughter as they experienced changes in communication choices and educational settings.

Listen With The Heart: Relationships And Hearing Loss by M. Harvey, San Diego, Dawn Sign Press, 2001.
This book describes the unique challenges of living with a hearing loss. Although many of the stories are about adults, we can learn from the experiences of the individuals who grew up deaf or hard of hearing.

The New Language Of Toys: Teaching Communication Skills To Children With Special Needs: A Guide For Parents And Teachers by S. Schwartz, & J.E.H. Miller, Bethesda, Woodbine, 1996.
This is a guide for parents of ways to use toys and everyday household items to help promote communication development in children.

Beyond Baby Talk: From Sounds to Sentences, A Parent's Complete Guide to Language Development by K. Apel & J. Masterson, American Speech and Hearing Association, 2001.
This book published by the American Speech and Hearing Association provides current information about effective ways parents can encourage speech and language development.

Kid-friendly Parenting With Deaf And Hard Of Hearing Children by D. Medwid & D.C. Weston, Gallaudet Press, Washington, DC. 1996.
This book addresses many issues that concern parents such as managing behaviour, how to set limits, helping children develop social skills, and dealing with school problems.

The Silent Garden: Raising Your Deaf Child, P. Ogden, Gallaudet University Press, Washington, DC, (revised 1996).
The Silent Garden provides the reader with important background information about deafness, describes various communication options, and provides case studies and interviews with parents.

WEBSITES, ORGANIZATIONS, NEWSLETTERS

BC Family Hearing Resource Centre
http://www.bcfamilyhearing.com
This is the website for the BC Family Hearing Resource Centre. You can connect with other parents, read current and past newsletter articles, and obtain up-to-date information on this website. Families and children can choose from a variety of communication options and strategies.

Boys Town National Research Hospital
http://www.babyhearing.org
We highly recommend this website for parents of young children with a hearing loss. This website is user-friendly and provides current information and support to parents.

Hands and Voices
http://www.handsandvoices.org
Hands & Voices is an excellent, non-profit organization dedicated to providing unbiased information and support to families who have deaf and hard of hearing children and to the professionals working with these families. You can sign up for their newsletter called "The Communicator."

Beginnings for Parents of Children Who Are Deaf or Hard of Hearing
http://www.beginningssvcs.com
This non-profit organization says their mission is to "help parents be informed, empowered and supported as they make decisions about their child." Beginnings does not promote any particular communication approach. This site provides some basic information on topics such as early intervention and Individualized Family Service Plans.

Alexander Graham Bell Association for the Deaf and Hard of Hearing (AG Bell)

http://www.agbell.org

This non-profit association promotes oral communication and oral education of deaf and hard of hearing individuals. Members can order the magazine "Voices" which publishes articles related to oral deafness.

John Tracy Clinic

http://www.jtc.org/

This organization provides free correspondence courses for parents of children with a hearing loss. Three-week summer sessions for children who are deaf and hard of hearing ages 2 through 5 years old and their families are also offered each summer at the Los Angeles campus. John Tracy Clinic focuses on the development of spoken language.

National Deaf Education Centre, Gallaudet University

http://clerccenter.gallaudet.edu/infotogo

The Laurent Clerc National Deaf Education Center (Clerc Center) at Gallaudet University has two demonstration schools for deaf students and works in collaboration with other professionals to conduct research in the area of deafness and provide training throughout the United States. This site provides lists of resources, organizations and website links related to deafness.

Canadian Hard of Hearing Association

http://www.chha.ca

The Canadian Hard of Hearing Association (CHHA) is an organization that is run by and for hard of hearing individuals. CHHA publishes an excellent magazine called "Listen/Écoute." Highlights of current and past issues of "Listen/Ecoute" are available on their website.

Canadian Hard of Hearing Association — BC Parents' Branch

http://www.chhaparents.bc.ca

CHHA - BC Parents' Branch is a province wide network of parents, families and friends of hard of hearing children. They organize annual conferences and publish a newsletter that is full of useful information for parents. Current and past issues of their newsletter are available on their website.

Family Network for Deaf Children — BC

http://www.fndc.ca

This is a British Columbia organization for families with deaf and hard of hearing children who use sign language as their primary language. They provide information and support to parents through workshops, videos, and an informative newsletter that is available on their website.

Canadian Association of the Deaf

http://www.cad.ca

This is the national consumer organization of Deaf Canadian citizens who use sign language as their primary language. Current and past issues of their newsletter, "CADChat" is available on their website.

American Society for Deaf Children

http://www.deafchildren.org

ASDC is a U.S. non-profit organization that provides support and information to families raising children who are deaf or hard of hearing. One of their primary focuses is to promote meaningful and full communication access, particularly through the competent use of sign language, in children's homes, schools and communities. This website has an extensive list of links related to deafness as well as a section called "Snapshots" which provides handouts on a range of topics of interest to parents.

Hearing Loss Association of America

http://www.hearingloss.org

Formerly called Self-Help for Hard of Hearing People (SHHH), the Hearing Loss Association of America is an organization in the United States for people with hearing loss. They publish a bimonthly magazine, "Hearing Loss". This organization also has a division that is focused on people who use cochlear implants.

Ski-Hi

http://www.coe.usu.edu/skihi

The Ski-Hi Institute has developed many good materials for service providers and families with children who have a hearing loss.

Raising Deaf Kids - Children's Hospital of Philadelphia

http://www.raisingdeafkids.org

This website has a comprehensive list of links related to hearing loss.

Auditory-Verbal International

http://www.auditory-verbal.org/

Auditory-Verbal International, Inc ® is a private, non-profit organization whose principal objective is to promote listening and speaking for children who are deaf or hard of hearing. This website has a parents' page where parents can post their personal webpage information; however parent webpages are only accepted on this site if they promote the auditory-verbal approach.

National Cued Speech Organization

http://www.cuedspeech.org

The National Cued Speech Association is a non-profit organization that promotes the effective use of Cued Speech. Cued Speech is a sound based visual communication system that uses handshapes and mouth movements to make the sounds of spoken language look different.

CDC - Early Hearing Detection and Intervention
http://www.cdc.gov/ncbddd/ehdi
This site provides links to up-to-date research related to infant hearing loss.

American Sign Language Browser
http://commtechlab.msu.edu/sites/aslwcb/index.htm
This Michigan State University website contains an online browser that allows you to look up videos demonstrating thousands of American Sign Language Signs.

Listen-Up
http://www.listen-up.org
This site was started by the mother of a child with a profound hearing loss. Although this website sells books and therapy materials for parents, it also has free helpful information, a list-service to help connect parents, as well as extensive links to other helpful websites.

SOURCES FOR ORDERING SIGN LANGUAGE VIDEOS/ BOOKS/DVDS

Harvard Medical School Center for Hereditary Deafness
http://hearing.harvard.edu/
Parents can find useful information about hereditary hearing loss and deafness, genetic testing, and causes of hearing loss. User friendly booklets that make genetics understandable are also available on this site.

Communicating With Your Child
This is an introduction to using some signed words and phrases based on first words that children typically understand and use at home. Signs are first demonstrated by a Deaf instructor, and then used in real life home situations by parents with their young Deaf and Hard of Hearing children. This is a wonderful resource for families who are starting to learn sign language. Available in VHS and DVD format. This video can be ordered at

BC Family Hearing Resource Centre
http://www.bcfamilyhearing.com
15220 92nd Avenue
Surrey, BC V3R 2T8
Phone: 604-584-2827
Fax: 604-584-2800
TTY: 604-584-9108

Boys Town Press
http://www.boystownpress.org
14100 Crawford Street
Boys Town, NE 68010
Toll-free 1-800-282-6657

Dawn Sign Press
http://www.dawnsign.com
6130 Nancy Ridge Drive
San Diego, CA 92121-3223
Phone: 858-625-0600
Fax: 858-625-2336

Gallaudet University Press
http://gupress.gallaudet.edu
800 Florida Avenue, NE
Washington, DC 20002
Phone: 202-651-5488 (voice/tty)

Baby Hands Productions
http://www.mybabycantalk.com
Baby Hands Productions, Inc.
Phone: 888-688-8008
Fax: 831-438-0922

Garlic Sign Press
http://www.garlicpress.com
1312 Jeppesen Avenue
Eugene, OR 97401
Phone: 541-345-0063
Fax: 541-683-8767

Hope, Inc.
Ski-Hi materials
http://www.hopepubl.com
1856 North 1200 East
North Logan, UT 84341
Phone: 435-245-2888

PARENT-TO-PARENT SUPPORT NETWORK

When a child is diagnosed with a hearing loss, the parents often want to talk with other parents of deaf and hard of hearing children. Through a parent support network, the BC Family Hearing Resource Centre have established a means for parents of deaf and hard of hearing children throughout BC to have contact with one another.

Parents tell us that their own friends and neighbours often do not really know what it is like to have a child who is deaf or hard of hearing. These parents found it helpful to have the opportunity to share experiences, concerns, and ideas with other families in similar situations.

WHY A SUPPORT NETWORK?

From a parent:

> *"When our child was first diagnosed, we felt so isolated. It seemed as if we were the only family in the world with a deaf child. The family we met through the support network helped us so much. They understood what we were going through. They had experienced similar frustrations with their child's behaviour before he was able to express himself. Now, John and I no longer feel so alone."*

From a parent:

> *"This was one of the most positive experiences we've had in dealing and coping with our child's hearing loss. We had never before seen another child wearing hearing aids! The other parents understood our worries and questions and were able to give us many useful tips."*

FOR MORE INFORMATION:

BCFHRC Parent-to-Parent Support Network
c/o BC Family Hearing Resource Centre
15220 92nd Avenue
Surrey, BC V3R 2T8
Canada
(604) 584-2827 (Voice)
(604) 584-9108 (TTY)
(604) 584-2800 (Fax)

SERVICES AVAILABLE FROM THE BC FAMILY HEARING RESOURCE CENTRE

- Parent-to-Parent Support Network
- Monthly newsletter with information and support for parents and professionals
- Resource Library
- Training programs for professionals working with deaf and hard of hearing children
- Ongoing consultation to families and professionals
- Speech, language, auditory learning
- Parent Support Group
- Home-based programs
- Preschool for deaf and hard of hearing children
- Sibling program
- Home sign language instruction
- Workshops for Early Childhood Educators
- Evening group sign language classes
- Support and information for extended family members

GLOSSARY

WORD	WHAT IT MEANS
ABR Test	Auditory Brainstem Evoked Response Test. It tests the response of your child's auditory nerve and the auditory area of the brain. Young children are usually sleeping or sedated for this test. Electrode stickers placed on your child's scalp record changes in the activity of the brainstem when sounds are presented to each ear through a headphone.
Atresia	Lack of an ear canal opening where sound normally travels by air waves to the middle ear. Atresia results in a conductive hearing loss.
Audiogram	A chart or graph that shows how well a person hears. It often shows what a person can hear with a hearing aid and without a hearing aid.
Audiologist	A person who tests hearing and works with deaf and hard of hearing individuals. Most audiologists have, as a minimum, a Master's degree and are certified by the Canadian Association of Speech-Language Pathologists and Audiologists. (In the United States, audiologists are certified by the American Speech-Language-Hearing Association.)
Audiometer	Electronic equipment that is used to test hearing.

Auditory Nerve	The hearing nerve that connects the cochlea to the brain. It sends messages from the ear to the brain.
Auditory Neuropathy	The child's external, middle, and inner ear or cochlea seems to receive sounds normally, but signals leaving the cochlea may be disorganized or the auditory nerve might not be processing sound normally. A child with auditory neuropathy often has more difficulty understanding speech than would be expected from his audiogram. The child's hearing may also seem to fluctuate.
Bilateral Hearing Loss	Hearing loss in both ears.
Bone-Anchored Hearing Aid (BAHA)	The BAHA is for children who benefit from bone conduction hearing aids. The BAHA contains a tiny box with a microphone, processor, and a battery, which are all attached to a titanium screw inserted into the skull. Sound vibrations are transmitted directly through the screw to the bone and from there to the cochlea.
Bone-Conduction Testing	A bone vibrator is placed behind the child's ear. The vibrator stimulates the inner ear directly and bypasses the middle ear. This helps to determine where the child's hearing problem is located. If the problem is located in the outer or middle ear (conductive hearing loss), then it may be helped with medical intervention. If the problem is located in the inner ear (the auditory nerve, or the auditory area of the brain), then it is a permanent type of hearing loss (sensorineural).
Bone Oscillator	The vibrator used in bone-conduction testing.

BTE hearing aids	Behind-the-ear hearing aids.
Cochlea	Forms the inner ear. It is a spiral-shaped bony casing that has many tiny nerve endings inside.
Cochlear Implant	A surgically implanted electronic device that bypasses damaged structures in the inner ear and directly stimulates the auditory nerve, allowing some deaf children to learn to hear and interpret sounds and speech.
Comfort Level (C Level)	The Maximum Comfort Level is the highest electrical stimulation level that does not produce an uncomfortable sensation for a child using a cochlear implant.
Conditioned Play Audiometry (CPA)	Child responds to sound by performing an action (for instance, putting a block in a bucket or a peg in a pegboard) immediately after he detects a sound.
Conductive Hearing Loss	Something is wrong with the outer ear - for instance, no opening to the ear canal. Problems with the middle ear can be the result of fluid in the middle ear - or there can be something wrong with the three little bones in the middle ear. Sometimes a conductive hearing loss is temporary when it is the kind of problem that can be medically treated.
Congenital Hearing Loss	A hearing loss present at birth or associated with the birth process, or which develops in the first few days of life.

Decibels (dB)

Intensity (loudness) of sound is measured in decibels. For instance, 100 dB is a very loud sound, and 10 dB is a very quiet sound.

Dynamic Range

A hearing loss present at birth or associated with the birth process, or which develops in the first few days of life.

Electrode Array

The internally worn part of the cochlear implant device. The array is inserted surgically into the cochlea. Electrodes along the array are activated to transmit high-pitch and low-pitch information to the auditory nerve.

Eardrum

The eardrum is situated between the outer ear and the inner ear. It is a membrane, or piece of skin, that covers a small opening in the ear. If your child has "tubes," these were inserted in the eardrum.

ENT

A doctor who is an Ear, Nose, and Throat Specialist.

Frequency/Pitch of Sound

Frequency is measured in Hertz (Hz). For instance, 250 Hz is a low frequency (or pitch) sound, and 4,000 Hz is a high frequency sound.

Hearing Threshold

The quietest sounds that a person can only barely hear. Aided threshold means the quietest sounds a person can just barely hear with his hearing aids on.

Impedance Testing	A small probe is placed in your child's ear. This test helps to decide what kind of hearing loss your child has (conductive or sensorineural). Impedance testing gives the audiologist information about: (1) flexibility of the eardrum, (2) middle ear pressure, (3) functioning of the middle ear bones, (4) functioning of the Eustachian tube, and (5) the reflex contraction of a small muscle in the middle ear.
Inner Ear	The part of the ear that contains the cochlea and the auditory nerve.
Localized	Child turns his head towards a sound.
MAP	The "listening program" stored in the memory of the cochlear implant processor.
Middle Ear	The middle section of the ear that contains three tiny bones, through which sound is conducted from the eardrum to the inner ear. This is where ear infections are usually located.
Mild Hearing Loss	A child is unable to detect sounds until they are in the loudness range of 26 dB to 40 dB.
Moderate Hearing Loss	A child is unable to detect sounds until they are in the loudness range of 41 dB to 55 dB.
Moderately Severe Hearing Loss	A child is unable to detect sounds until they are in the loudness range of 56 dB to 70 dB.

Otitis Media	An infection in the middle ear which can result in a temporary slight-to-moderate hearing loss. Fluid build-up without a current infection may also cause a temporary hearing loss. Children who already have a permanent sensorineural hearing loss need the advantage of every bit of hearing available to them. For this reason, parents of deaf and hard of hearing children who suffer from chronic ear infections should seek help from a specialist (otologist).
Otoacoustic Emissions	A sensitive microphone is placed in the child's ear while the audiologist presents several "clicks" or "tones." If the child's cochlea is normal, an echo of the clicks or tones comes back and is recorded. The absence of an echo may indicate a hearing loss, and the child then receives further hearing tests.
Outer Ear	The visible part of the ear that we can see, as well as the ear canal, which channels sound from outside through to the eardrum.
Profound Hearing Loss	Child is unable to detect sounds until they are 90 dB or louder.
Sensorineural Hearing Loss	Something is wrong with the inner ear (for instance nerve endings in cochlea are damaged). This is a permanent type of hearing loss.
Severe Hearing Loss	Child is unable to detect sounds until they are in the loudness range of 71 dB to 90 dB.

Single-Sided Deafness (SSD)	The term given to unilateral sensorineural deafness.
Slight Hearing Loss	A child is unable to detect sounds until they are in the loudness level of 15 to 25 dB.
Sloping Hearing Loss	A child's hearing loss is not the same across all frequencies (pitch). In most cases, a child with a sloping hearing loss has better hearing in the lower frequencies than in the higher frequencies. On such a child's audiogram (graph), you would see a sloping downward line that connects the symbols (X, O or > and <) which mark the loudness of sounds heard at different pitches.
Sound Field	Sound is presented through loud speakers. Testing in sound field tells us what the child can hear with his better ear.
Speech Awareness Threshold	The quietest level at which the child detects speech 50% of the time. This is tested by the audiologist.
Speech Banana	Shows the loudness level of speech sounds on an audiogram.
Speech Discrimination Test	Shows how well a child hears the different vowel and consonant sounds in words. This is most often used with a child who has developed speech and oral language.

Speech Reception Threshold Test	Shows how loud speech must be before a child can understand words spoken by the audiologist. The audiologist may ask the child to point to familiar toys or pictures of objects. For example, "Show me the airplane."
Threshold Level (T level)	The minimum level of electrical stimulation required at each electrode along the cochlear implant electrode array for a child to first hear a sound.
Tympanogram	The results of tympanometry testing (mobility of the eardrum) are recorded on a graph or chart. A graph with a flat line indicates middle ear problems such as presence of fluid (no mobility). A graph with a curve like a mountain indicates normal mobility.
Tympanometry Testing	A small probe is placed in your child's ear while the movement of the eardrum is measured. This test shows if there is a problem in the middle ear, such as middle ear fluid which may accompany or follow an ear infection.
Unilateral Hearing Loss	Person has a hearing loss in only one ear.
Visual Reinforced Audiometry (VRA)	A toy that lights up and moves (for instance, a toy monkey that claps his hands) as soon as a child indicates in some way that he is aware of a sound (such as a tone) that has been presented. The child learns that when he responds to sound, he is then rewarded or reinforced with the moving toy.

A PARENT'S JOURNAL

JACKSON G.
- cochlear implant surgery: June 19 (13 months old)
- turn-on: July 17-18 (14 months old)

COCHLEAR IMPLANT HOOKUP (14 MONTHS OLD)

July 17

J. cried when his cochlear implant was turned on with all of us talking to him. He wouldn't stop crying and I think he was experiencing a sensation he had never had before. It was very emotional.

August 2

J. turned to Rock n Roll Elmo doll! Whenever doll plays, he stops what he's doing and turns to find Elmo! J. will pick airplane out of "toy-sound bucket" when he hears us say "ahhhh" sound.

August 8

J. hears cars on the street outside; he points to the road when cars go by, even when not looking in that direction, when the front door is open. He definitely hears the toilet flush (I think for a while now) and it seems to scare him a bit.

August 9

J. hears the phone! He turns to the ring even when not looking in that direction.

August 14

J. heard Great Auntie Susan say "cock-a-doodle-doo"!

August 16

J. holds the toy airplane and flies the plane around and says "ah"!

1 MONTH POST-IMPLANT (15 MONTHS OLD)

August 24

J. hears Dad call "Jackson" fairly consistently; when he asks "Find La La" J. will go and get La La doll. He also points to the bathroom and comes to find me when the hairdryer is turned on. Hears all kinds of sounds in the house such as the toaster bell and the microwave beeping.

September 8

J. is understanding words! We went to Maplewood Farm and when we came home I said "Tell Daddy you saw ducks – quack quack". Then J. made the sign for "duck" without me giving any visual clues! He also makes the "m" sound for "cow", and when I say "moo" he goes and gets the toy cow. New sound: popping sounds with his mouth.

September 10

I suspect J. understands the words cow, shoe, up, light on, and ball??

September 13

J. understands cow ("moo") and train ("choo choo").

2 MONTHS POST IMPLANT (16 MONTHS OLD)

September 17

J. has stopped pulling off the implant coil; we think he has made the connection that it is how he hears.

September 19

definitely understands and will wave when we say "bye-bye". Dancing to musical toys a lot. "Talks" on toy phone – "uh huh, mmm". Makes "huh huh huh" sounds for pig oinking.

J's magnet (coil) came off when playing on the couch. He reached up to his ear on the opposite side – this is the first time he's made the connection between the magnet and his hearing!

September 20

When we said "Where's Po? Go get Po" (we were in the living room and Po was on the kitchen floor), J. went over to Po and picked him up! (We didn't point or look at Po)

When J. stands close to the light switch I say "J., turn the light off/on" and he will turn it off or on. I tried this instruction when he was facing the other direction from me and he turned right around and flipped the switch.

We think he understands the words "push", and "throw" because we use these words with different activities and he does the action.

September 21

When Tim said "Where are your eyes?" J. pointed to his eyes (several different times that day).

September 23

J. saw the collapsible dog on the TV cabinet. He went "huh huh", and then I collapsed it. He repeated this about 8 or 10 times; each time with him saying "huh huh" for "woof woof", as I have said it to him before. This is the first clear time that he was using his voice to cause an action (besides wanting to be picked up).

September 24

I put a picture of a cow up on the fridge. J. loved it. He continually pointed to it, touched it, and said "mmm mm" throughout the afternoon and evening.

September 25

J. saw a cat while walking with Nana and she said he made "mm ma meh" sounds.

September 26

J. pulled out a cat book from a stack of other books and said "meow" or something very close to that!! He is making some different noises today – not sure how to describe them – "p", "b", "d" maybe? Lots of humming while in the toy car.

October 3

consistently says "uh uh" for "up" when he wants to be picked up. I spent yesterday writing down the words he knows – some I'm 100% sure he understands, others I'm pretty sure. J. is making new sounds a lot: "oo", "ee", "duh", "nuh".

October 9

Uses "b" sound in "ba ba", "oh", and "i".

October 10

Tim and J. play the "cough game"; he coughs, Tim coughs back, and it continues. J. thinks this is very funny. Clapping (for an audience) a lot, then we clap and say "yea".

October 15

J. always wants his processor and headset on as soon as he sees it upon waking or from in the bath.

3 MONTHS POST IMPLANT (17 MONTHS OLD)

October 19

Says "ee ee" for *mouse*, "aw" for *on* and *off* (light), "haw haw" for *bunnies hopping*, "aaa" for *sheep*, "uh" for *duck*

October 31

Understands "hot" and says "ha" for *stove, heater, coffee cups, candles, Jack-o-Lantern,* and *fire*.

November 1

Babbles all day long. Makes a new sound by breathing in, as if he is experimenting with how he can talk and get attention.

November 2

Plays the "wake up game" by using his voice to wake me up when I am pretending to sleep.

November 10

Understands so many phrases ("Put it in the garbage", "Say bye-bye", "Go and get the mail") and words (*jump, Mommy/ Daddy, crayons, cookie, book, piano, blanket, water, juice, milk*).

LEARNING TO LISTEN AND COMMUNICATE
— FROM A CHILD'S POINT OF VIEW

Yes, the little tot is me. Real tiny, wasn't I? But I have lots more hair now :)

My name is Rosalind Ho. I was born with a severe hearing loss that sharply declined to profound when I was 3 years old. I received a cochlear implant just before I turned four.

My parents chose to enroll me at the Elks Family Hearing Resource Centre (now the BC Family Hearing Resource Centre) because of its family-centered approach. Each family finds the best method of communication that works for the family and especially for the child, and the Centre provides as much support as they can.

My parents used a total communication approach in teaching me language because they didn't believe the myth that learning to sign would impede my speech and English language development. The most important thing to my family was to be able to communicate with each other.

I always thought that this was the best approach that could be used. Receiving the cochlear implant plus years of intensive rehab and speech therapy helped me learn to hear and speak fluent English. Signs helped me understand the sounds I heard. For example, if I hear the word "book" (my absolute favourite word in the world) then I connect it to the sign "book". Visual cues help me navigate the world around me because my hearing isn't perfect, even with a CI.

Today, I am fluent in both English and American Sign Language. I love to read — when the fourth, fifth, and sixth *Harry Potter* books came out, I stayed up until about 4 a.m. to finish them — it drove my parents nuts! My next favourite books are *The Jade Peony* and *All That Matters* by Wayson Choy. I enjoy them because they are about second-generation Chinese kids growing up in Canada, just like me.

In June I will be graduating from Burnaby South Secondary and the BC Provincial School for the Deaf. I have already been accepted to several universities with entrance scholarships, including University of British Columbia and Simon Fraser Univesity. I plan to major in English and become a journalist or writer so that I can fulfill my lifelong passion of advocating for the rights of people with hearing loss.

These days, I'm up to my eyeballs studying for my Advanced Placement exams in May and the Provincial Exams in June. But, my community and especially the BC Family Hearing Resource Centre has given me so many boosts in life, that I feel that I should give something back, despite my busy life. Which is why I am sharing my story with you. I hope you enjoyed it. Don't forget, just because a child is deaf does not prevent them from going out there to smell the roses and give the sun a run for his money.

Gotta go study now, and I'm sure I'll see you around sometime soon. Take care :)

Rosalind Ho

April 1, 2006